Water Conservation: Improving Water Efficiency and Water Management for Sustainable Agriculture, Urban Water Use, Industrial Water Recycling, Water Policy, and Climate Resilience

Copyright

Water Conservation: Improving Water Efficiency and Water Management for Sustainable Agriculture, Urban Water Use, Industrial Water Recycling, Water Policy, and Climate Resilience

The author and publisher are of the same opinion regarding the views and content expressed in this work.

Disclaimer: The information in this book is provided for general knowledge and educational purposes only. While every effort has been made to ensure accuracy, the author and publisher make no representations or warranties with respect to the completeness or suitability of the content. The author and publisher accept no liability for any errors, omissions, or outcomes resulting from the application of information contained herein. Readers are advised to consult appropriate professionals or authorities before acting on any material presented.

ISBN (eBook): 978-1-991370-84-6

ISBN (Paperback): 978-1-991370-85-3

Published by Our Future Water

First Edition, 2025

Cover design and interior layout by Our Future Water

Table of Contents

Introduction

Water is the foundation of all life and a critical driver of social and economic development. Yet, as the global population rises, cities expand, industries grow, and the impacts of climate change intensify, ensuring sustainable access to clean, reliable water has emerged as one of the defining challenges of our era. Across continents, water stress is becoming the new normal, manifesting in dwindling rivers, overdrawn aquifers, recurring droughts, and mounting competition among users. The urgency to use water more efficiently, conserve what we have, and build resilience against uncertainty is now clearer than ever.

This book explores the essential role of water conservation and efficiency in safeguarding the future. It recognizes that water is not just an environmental concern, but a shared asset underpinning food security, energy production, industrial growth, urban well-being, and ecosystem health. While the challenges are immense and complex, solutions are within reach. Success depends on the coordinated efforts of governments, utilities, businesses, farmers, engineers, and communities, all empowered by data, policy, and innovation.

Water Conservation: Improving Water Efficiency and Water Management for Sustainable Agriculture, Urban Water Use, Industrial Water Recycling, Water Policy, and Climate Resilience provides a comprehensive guide to understanding and implementing water-saving measures across the full spectrum of society. Each chapter unpacks the unique dynamics, barriers, and opportunities in key sectors, energy, agriculture, public supply, industry, mining, and construction, while highlighting best practices in monitoring, governance, policy, and stakeholder engagement. By bridging sectoral divides and focusing on practical solutions, this book aims to inspire integrated action for water security.

Ultimately, achieving sustainable water management will require a blend of technology, leadership, and collective responsibility. This book offers the strategies, insights, and inspiration needed to shape a future where water is valued, protected, and used wisely for generations to come.

Defining Water Conservation and Efficiency

Water conservation and efficiency are central to securing a sustainable future in the face of growing global pressures. Water conservation refers to strategies and actions aimed at reducing the overall use of water resources, either through behavioral changes or technological interventions that minimize waste. Efficiency, in contrast, is about maximizing the benefits derived from each unit of water consumed, ensuring that water is used in the most productive manner possible within any given process or sector. Both concepts are interconnected, as improved efficiency often leads to conservation, while conservation efforts can drive the adoption of more efficient technologies and practices. These dual approaches are crucial for maintaining the balance between human needs and the natural environment, especially as water scarcity intensifies in many regions.

Drivers of Rising Water Demand Across Sectors

Rising water demand is a consequence of multiple, overlapping trends across sectors worldwide. Rapid population growth and urbanization place increasing pressure on municipal water supplies, requiring more water for household use, sanitation, and expanding urban landscapes. In agriculture, intensification and the drive to feed a growing global population escalate irrigation and processing needs, especially in arid and semi-arid regions. Industrial development, along with the expansion of energy production and resource extraction, brings about significant increases in water withdrawal and consumption for manufacturing, cooling, and mining activities. Additionally, changing lifestyles, tourism growth, and service sector expansion further heighten water use in cities and resorts. These drivers are compounded by climate variability, which alters rainfall patterns, increases evapotranspiration, and amplifies the challenge of meeting demand with available supply. Addressing these pressures requires coordinated, sector-wide efforts to improve water conservation and efficiency.

Objectives and Scope of the Book

This book aims to provide a comprehensive, cross-sectoral examination of water conservation and efficiency strategies, equipping stakeholders with the knowledge required to address today's water challenges and build resilience for the future. The content is structured to cover the full spectrum of water use, spanning thermoelectric and renewable power generation, agriculture, public water supply, industry, mining, and construction, each with its unique patterns, demands, and opportunities for improvement. Central to this examination are the latest advances in monitoring, performance metrics, policy instruments, and institutional arrangements, as well as the vital roles of stakeholders and the necessity of adapting to climate risks. Readers will gain insights into the specific drivers of water use within each sector, practical approaches for reducing waste and optimizing efficiency, and tools for measuring, benchmarking, and reporting progress. The book is designed for policymakers, practitioners, industry professionals, and researchers who seek actionable guidance and integrated strategies. Ultimately, it calls for innovative thinking and coordinated action to ensure water resources are managed wisely, enabling both economic development and environmental sustainability in a changing world.

Chapter 1 – Water Use and Efficiency in Thermoelectric and Renewable Power Generation

Energy and water are fundamentally interconnected, with the production of electricity, whether from fossil fuels, nuclear, or renewable sources, relying heavily on water for cooling, steam generation, and a variety of other processes. As the demand for energy grows and the transition toward low-carbon sources accelerates, the efficient management of water in the power sector is increasingly critical for sustainability, cost control, and climate resilience.

Thermoelectric power plants, including coal, natural gas, and nuclear facilities, have historically been among the largest users of freshwater resources globally. These plants require substantial volumes of water for cooling and condensing steam, often resulting in significant withdrawals from rivers, lakes, or aquifers and creating challenges related to thermal pollution, water scarcity, and regulatory compliance. With aging infrastructure, tightening environmental regulations, and increasing competition for water from other sectors, the need to optimize water use in thermoelectric generation is more pressing than ever.

At the same time, the growth of renewable energy sources, such as wind, solar photovoltaics, and advanced storage technologies, offers a pathway to reducing the water footprint of electricity generation. Unlike traditional power plants, many renewables require little or no water for operation, presenting new opportunities for both decarbonization and water conservation. However, the transition to these technologies is not without challenges, including issues related to intermittency, integration, and the continued reliance on water-intensive processes in some emerging renewable systems.

This chapter provides a comprehensive overview of water use and efficiency across thermoelectric and renewable power generation. It explores the drivers of water demand, evaluates the water footprints of different technologies, highlights strategies for reducing consumption, and examines the future landscape of water-smart energy systems. By understanding these dynamics, stakeholders can make informed decisions that advance both energy security and water sustainability.

Water Demands in Power Generation

Power generation is among the largest users of water worldwide, with demand shaped by the scale, technology, and location of generation facilities. Water is vital not only for cooling purposes but also for steam generation, pollution control, and auxiliary services within plants. The electricity sector's water footprint has historically been dominated by thermoelectric power plants, which encompass coal, natural gas, oil, and nuclear technologies. These facilities require substantial volumes of water to absorb waste heat and maintain optimal operating conditions. In many countries, thermoelectric generation accounts for the majority of industrial water withdrawals, sometimes rivaling or surpassing agricultural use in water-stressed regions.

Thermoelectric power plants generally use water for two main purposes: cooling and steam production. Water is heated to produce steam that drives turbines, and after the steam passes through the turbines, it must be cooled and condensed back into water before being reused or discharged. This cooling process, whether through open-cycle (once-through), closed-cycle (recirculating), or hybrid systems, determines the overall volume of water required and the share of that water that is ultimately consumed (evaporated) or returned to the source. Once-through cooling, while requiring high withdrawal rates, results in relatively low water consumption as most water is returned, albeit at higher temperatures and potentially altered chemical composition. Recirculating or closed-cycle systems withdraw less water but consume a higher proportion, as more is lost to evaporation in cooling towers.

The intensity of water demand in power generation is not uniform and varies widely by technology, scale, and local climatic conditions. For example, nuclear and coal-fired plants are typically more water-intensive due to their higher steam cycle temperatures and continuous cooling needs. Gas-fired plants can be less demanding, particularly in combined cycle configurations, but still contribute significantly to local water demand. The availability and quality of water sources also influence plant siting, design, and operation, with some facilities relying on rivers, lakes, groundwater, or even municipal supplies.

Beyond cooling and steam generation, power plants also use water for emissions scrubbing, ash handling, flue gas desulfurization, and other ancillary processes. The quality of water required may vary, from high-purity boiler feedwater to raw or recycled water for cooling or cleaning. As environmental standards tighten, water demand for pollution control and compliance can also increase, adding to the sector's overall footprint.

The growing integration of renewable energy sources introduces a new dimension to the water-power nexus. Hydropower, while often promoted as a clean energy source, can significantly alter natural flow regimes and impact downstream water availability. Wind and solar photovoltaic (PV) technologies, by contrast, require minimal water during operation but may still involve water use in manufacturing, cleaning, and site maintenance. The trend toward decarbonization and energy diversification raises important questions about the water implications of different power sector pathways and the need to balance energy security with water sustainability.

Population growth, urbanization, and industrialization are expanding electricity demand, placing additional pressure on already stressed water resources. Climate change adds further complexity, with shifting precipitation patterns, droughts, and heatwaves altering water availability at precisely the times when electricity demand for cooling and other uses is likely to rise. The challenge for policymakers, utilities, and industry is to navigate these intersecting pressures by adopting technologies and practices that deliver both energy and water efficiency gains, ultimately supporting long-term system resilience.

Effective management of water in power generation requires a holistic approach, integrating resource planning, demand forecasting, technology selection, and site-specific assessments of water risk. Utilities and regulators are increasingly recognizing the value of comprehensive water-energy planning, which can identify synergies, trade-offs, and opportunities for conservation across the entire value chain. This chapter explores the principal dimensions of water use in the electricity sector, highlighting the critical role of cooling, the comparative footprints of different technologies, and the emerging opportunities for efficiency improvement and system transformation.

Thermoelectric Cooling Methods and Water Use

Cooling systems are central to thermoelectric power plants, determining both the total water withdrawn and the proportion consumed. The choice of cooling technology, once-through, recirculating, dry, or hybrid, affects the plant's operational efficiency, environmental impact, and long-term viability, particularly in regions facing water scarcity or competing demands.

Once-through cooling is the most traditional approach, drawing large volumes of water from a nearby source, passing it through heat exchangers to absorb waste heat, and then returning it to the environment at a higher temperature. This method is highly effective in terms of thermal efficiency and relatively inexpensive to install and operate. However, it requires the highest withdrawal rates of all cooling options and can result in significant thermal pollution, negatively affecting aquatic ecosystems and local water temperatures. Environmental regulations in many regions are now limiting or phasing out once-through systems due to these impacts.

Recirculating or closed-cycle cooling systems use the same water repeatedly, circulating it through cooling towers where heat is dissipated to the atmosphere. These systems withdraw far less water than once-through designs but consume more, as a portion evaporates during cooling. While recirculating systems can significantly reduce the pressure on local water bodies, they require a steady supply to compensate for evaporative losses and can be more complex and costly to operate. Advances in cooling tower technology, such as improved materials and designs, are helping to optimize performance and reduce both water and energy consumption.

Dry cooling represents the lowest water use option, employing air-cooled condensers instead of water-based systems. This approach dramatically cuts water withdrawals and virtually eliminates consumption, making it attractive in arid or water-stressed regions. However, dry cooling is generally less efficient, particularly in hot climates, as air cannot absorb heat as effectively as water. This can reduce plant output and increase operating costs, presenting a trade-off between water conservation and thermal efficiency.

Hybrid cooling systems combine elements of wet and dry cooling to provide greater flexibility and resilience. During periods of water abundance, wet cooling is used for maximum efficiency, while dry cooling can be deployed during droughts or peak demand to reduce water consumption. Hybrid systems are becoming more common in areas with variable water availability or where regulatory requirements demand stringent water use reductions.

The selection of cooling technology is influenced by a range of factors, including local water availability, regulatory constraints, plant size and location, cost considerations, and broader system integration needs. In regions facing tightening water supplies, the trend is toward adoption of recirculating, hybrid, or dry cooling systems, supported by regulatory incentives or mandates. Utilities and developers must balance operational efficiency, capital and maintenance costs, and environmental stewardship in choosing the most appropriate cooling approach.

In summary, cooling technology selection has a direct and profound impact on the overall water demand of thermoelectric power generation. As environmental regulations become more stringent and water scarcity intensifies, power plant operators will need to increasingly prioritize water-efficient cooling solutions that align with both system performance goals and sustainability objectives.

Water Footprint of Fossil, Nuclear, and Renewables

Understanding the water footprint of different power generation technologies is crucial for informed resource planning and decision-making. The water footprint includes all water used in the lifecycle of electricity generation, from extraction and processing of fuels to plant operation and cooling, through to decommissioning and remediation.

Fossil fuel-based power plants, including coal, oil, and natural gas, tend to have the largest operational water footprints due to the significant volumes required for steam production, cooling, emissions control, and ash handling. Coal-fired power plants, in particular, are among the most water-intensive, especially those employing once-through cooling. Water is also used upstream in mining, washing, and transport of coal. Natural gas plants, especially in combined cycle configurations, are generally more efficient and less water-intensive but still contribute to cumulative water demand.

Nuclear power presents a similar water profile to coal, as both rely on steam cycle technologies. Nuclear plants require highly reliable, large-scale cooling systems for both safety and operational efficiency. Water use can be reduced with closed-cycle or dry cooling, but these adaptations may come with higher costs or lower thermal efficiency. Water demand for uranium mining and processing is also part of the nuclear lifecycle footprint.

Renewable energy technologies have a more diverse range of water footprints. **Hydropower** requires large volumes for reservoir creation and management, with significant implications for river systems and downstream users. However, water is not typically consumed but stored and released, except for evaporation from reservoirs, which can be substantial in arid regions. **Geothermal** plants, depending on their design, can have significant water needs for cooling and for managing geothermal fluids, but many are shifting to air-cooling or closed-loop systems to limit withdrawals.

Wind and solar PV technologies are the least water-intensive during operation, using negligible amounts for cleaning panels or routine maintenance. The primary water use is embedded in the manufacturing of components and, for solar thermal (concentrated solar power, CSP), in steam generation and cooling, though even here, dry or hybrid cooling systems can substantially reduce demand.

Bioenergy (including biofuels and biomass power) can have a significant water footprint, largely attributable to crop cultivation, irrigation, and processing. Lifecycle assessments reveal that bioenergy pathways must be carefully managed to avoid unintended consequences for water resources, especially where feedstock production competes with food or natural ecosystems.

As electricity systems transition toward decarbonization, the aggregate water footprint of the power sector is expected to decline, especially where wind, solar PV, and other low-water technologies displace fossil and nuclear generation. However, the pace and scale of this transition are highly variable, influenced by regional water availability, policy frameworks, and infrastructure readiness.

A nuanced understanding of water footprints is essential for effective policy, planning, and investment. Lifecycle assessment tools and reporting frameworks are increasingly being used to provide transparency and guide choices toward lower-impact, sustainable power generation pathways. As water becomes a more visible constraint in energy planning, the ability to compare and optimize water use across the full technology mix will be central to long-term system resilience.

Efficiency Gains in Cooling and Process Systems

Technological advances in cooling and process systems offer substantial opportunities to reduce water demand in power generation. Improving the efficiency of these systems not only conserves water but can also lower energy costs, enhance operational reliability, and support compliance with increasingly stringent environmental standards.

Cooling system efficiency is a major focus for utilities seeking to minimize water use. Upgrades to existing infrastructure, such as replacing aging cooling towers with higher-efficiency models, optimizing heat exchanger performance, and adopting advanced materials, can lead to meaningful water savings. Some plants have implemented variable-speed fans, high-efficiency drift eliminators, and improved fill media to enhance cooling performance while reducing evaporation losses.

The adoption of **hybrid cooling systems** represents a significant innovation, offering the flexibility to switch between wet and dry cooling based on water availability, ambient temperature, and demand conditions. This allows operators to reduce water consumption during droughts or high-stress periods while maintaining high efficiency when water is abundant. In regions with seasonal variability or regulatory constraints on water withdrawals, hybrid systems can provide a critical buffer, enhancing both operational flexibility and environmental performance.

Dry cooling technologies continue to improve, with advances in finned-tube design, improved air flow management, and automation enabling greater efficiency even in challenging climates. The integration of artificial intelligence and real-time monitoring is further optimizing the performance of air-cooled condensers, balancing the trade-offs between water conservation and plant output.

Process optimization within power plants also plays a key role in improving water efficiency. Advanced **water management systems** monitor usage, identify leaks or inefficiencies, and enable targeted interventions. The implementation of closed-loop process water systems, where water is captured, treated, and reused internally, is becoming more widespread, particularly in regions with high water costs or scarcity. Combined with digital controls, these systems can provide near real-time feedback to operators, supporting continuous improvement and compliance with reporting requirements.

Automation and digitalization are driving improvements in both cooling and process systems. The use of Supervisory Control and Data Acquisition (SCADA) systems, Internet of Things (IoT) sensors, and data analytics enables more precise control of water use, temperature, and flow rates. Predictive maintenance tools can identify and address potential problems before they lead to significant water loss or system downtime.

Water chemistry management is another critical aspect of process optimization. By maintaining proper water quality, operators can reduce scaling, corrosion, and fouling, which otherwise necessitate more frequent blowdown, higher makeup water volumes, and increased chemical use. Treatment technologies, such as ultrafiltration, reverse osmosis, and advanced ion exchange, support higher cycles of concentration, reducing the need for freshwater intake.

Emissions control systems, such as flue gas desulfurization and particulate removal, can also be optimized for water efficiency. Modern scrubbers and dry sorbent injection systems use less water while achieving high levels of pollutant removal, aligning environmental compliance with conservation objectives.

Collectively, these improvements in cooling and process systems form the foundation for water-smart power generation. Utilities that invest in efficiency not only reduce their exposure to water risk but also position themselves for success in a future shaped by tighter regulations, evolving market expectations, and the growing imperative for sustainable resource use.

Hybrid Cooling and Improved Tower Design

Hybrid cooling systems and advanced tower designs have emerged as key solutions for balancing water efficiency and thermal performance in power generation. By integrating wet and dry cooling components, hybrid systems enable flexible operation tailored to water availability, regulatory requirements, and operational priorities.

Hybrid cooling combines the strengths of traditional wet (evaporative) cooling and dry (air-cooled) systems. In wet mode, water is used to absorb heat and is partially evaporated, delivering high cooling efficiency. In dry mode, air is used to remove heat, dramatically reducing or eliminating water use. Operators can switch between modes or operate both simultaneously, optimizing for water conservation during scarcity or cost savings when water is readily available.

These systems are particularly valuable in regions with variable water availability or frequent droughts, where reliance on a single mode could compromise reliability or violate environmental permits. Hybrid cooling also supports compliance with seasonal or annual water use restrictions, providing a hedge against regulatory or supply risks.

Improved cooling tower design is central to maximizing the efficiency of both hybrid and recirculating systems. Advances include the use of corrosion-resistant materials, enhanced fill media to increase surface area and heat transfer, and improved drift eliminators to minimize water loss through fine mist. Variable-speed drives and intelligent controls further optimize fan and pump operation, reducing energy consumption while maintaining target temperatures.

Design innovations are also addressing environmental and community concerns. Noise reduction features, plume abatement technologies, and visual screening are now standard in many new installations, supporting community acceptance and regulatory compliance.

Retrofitting existing plants with improved tower designs and hybrid capabilities can deliver significant water and energy savings. Utilities are increasingly undertaking such upgrades as part of broader asset management and sustainability programs, often supported by regulatory incentives or performance-based standards.

The integration of hybrid cooling and advanced tower designs represents a practical pathway for power generators to meet growing demand while protecting local water resources. As climate variability intensifies and water scarcity becomes a defining constraint, these solutions are likely to become standard practice across the sector.

Process Water Reuse in Energy Systems

Process water reuse is an important strategy for reducing the overall water footprint of power generation. By capturing, treating, and reusing water within the plant, utilities can lower their demand for freshwater, reduce wastewater discharges, and improve operational resilience.

Internal water recycling can take many forms, from the reuse of cooling tower blowdown and boiler condensate to the recapture of process water from emissions control systems. Water that is no longer suitable for high-purity applications can often be reused in less demanding processes, creating a cascade of reuse opportunities that maximize each drop's utility.

Treatment technologies are critical enablers of process water reuse. Filtration, sedimentation, chemical precipitation, membrane systems (such as reverse osmosis or ultrafiltration), and advanced oxidation processes can remove impurities and condition water for reuse. In some cases, on-site treatment can bring wastewater up to potable or near-potable standards, opening new opportunities for high-value reuse.

Process water reuse not only reduces reliance on external supplies but can also cut operating costs, particularly where water purchase, transport, or treatment fees are high. It also helps plants meet increasingly strict effluent discharge standards, as less wastewater is released to the environment.

The design and operation of process water reuse systems must consider water chemistry, potential for scaling or fouling, compatibility with existing plant equipment, and regulatory requirements. Automated monitoring and control are essential for maintaining water quality and optimizing reuse rates.

Beyond the plant boundary, some power generators are engaging in **water-sharing arrangements** with neighboring industries, municipalities, or agricultural users, creating integrated water management solutions that benefit all parties. In these arrangements, treated process water or effluent from one facility is supplied for use in another, supporting broader community or industrial needs while conserving regional water resources.

In summary, process water reuse is a practical, cost-effective approach to reducing freshwater demand, improving environmental performance, and supporting the long-term sustainability of power generation.

Transitioning to Low-Water Energy Systems

The power sector's transition toward low-water energy systems is accelerating as utilities, regulators, and governments recognize the critical need to decouple electricity production from water consumption. This shift is driven by a combination of water scarcity, regulatory pressures, climate change, and the rapidly improving cost-competitiveness of alternative technologies.

Wind, Solar PV, and Other Water-Light Options

Wind power is among the most water-efficient forms of electricity generation available. Modern wind turbines require virtually no water for operation, only minimal amounts are used for periodic cleaning and lubrication. The primary water use is embedded in the manufacturing and construction of towers, blades, and foundations, but these are one-time inputs rather than ongoing operational demands. As wind power capacity expands globally, it is displacing water-intensive generation, especially in regions prone to drought or high water stress.

Solar PV technology is similarly advantageous from a water perspective. Once installed, solar panels require little more than occasional cleaning, often accomplished with rainwater or minimal manual washing. In desert or dusty regions, water use for cleaning can increase but remains negligible compared to cooling needs in thermoelectric plants. The broader adoption of robotic dry-cleaning and advanced panel coatings is further reducing water requirements.

Other low-water renewable options include geothermal plants with closed-loop or air-cooled designs, landfill gas, and tidal or wave energy. Each has specific water use profiles, but overall, these technologies are moving the sector toward minimal operational water use.

Importantly, as more variable renewables are added to the grid, the overall system becomes less dependent on water. However, careful planning is required to address the intermittency of wind and solar, ensuring that system reliability is maintained without reverting to water-intensive backup generation.

Role of Storage and Integration for Water Reduction

The increasing penetration of renewables requires robust storage and grid integration solutions to balance supply and demand. The water implications of these technologies are generally positive, but they require careful consideration in system planning.

Battery storage systems, such as lithium-ion, flow batteries, and emerging solid-state designs, have negligible operational water requirements. The principal water use is during manufacturing and recycling, but this is small compared to conventional generation. The widespread deployment of batteries allows for greater renewable penetration, smoothing fluctuations and reducing reliance on peaking plants that may be water-intensive.

Pumped hydro storage is a well-established grid balancing technology and remains the largest form of energy storage globally. While it uses water to move energy between upper and **lower reservoirs,** modern pumped hydro systems are typically closed-loop, meaning little water is lost except for minor evaporation. While initial construction alters local hydrology and requires significant water input, operational use is relatively stable and can complement renewables without major additional withdrawals. However, in water-scarce regions or drought-prone areas, even closed-loop pumped hydro requires careful site selection and management to avoid compounding water stress.

Thermal energy storage (such as molten salt for concentrated solar power) is another integration option. While CSP plants with thermal storage can have higher water requirements if they use wet cooling, using dry or hybrid cooling and closed-loop designs can keep operational water use low. Innovations in phase-change materials and dry-cooled CSP are further reducing water intensity, enabling broader deployment in arid zones.

Grid integration of renewables, batteries, and storage solutions allows utilities to reduce the "must-run" status of baseload fossil and nuclear plants, these are typically the most water-intensive. As systems become more flexible, operators can dispatch electricity based on both energy and water availability, adjusting output to coincide with periods of abundant water or shifting load to low-water sources during scarcity. Digitalization, real-time monitoring, and smart grid technologies enable this dynamic balancing, supporting both energy and water conservation objectives.

Demand-side management and distributed energy resources, including rooftop solar and local battery storage, can further cut system-wide water demand. By reducing peak loads and enabling more local supply, these strategies limit the need to run or build large, water-intensive power plants.

Looking Forward: The Water-Energy Transition

Transitioning to low-water energy systems is a central pillar of sustainable power sector development. The shift is driven by:

- **Policy and Regulation:** Increasingly stringent water-use regulations, environmental licensing, and integrated resource planning are compelling utilities to adopt water-smart technologies.
- **Economic Drivers:** The falling costs of renewables and storage, alongside rising costs for water procurement, treatment, and regulatory compliance, are tilting the balance in favor of low-water options.
- **Climate Change:** Droughts, heatwaves, and altered precipitation are intensifying the need to minimize dependence on water in power generation, particularly in regions already under stress.
- **Corporate Responsibility:** Utilities and developers are increasingly evaluated on ESG criteria, with water stewardship a critical dimension for investors and stakeholders.

The success of this transition hinges on systems thinking, technological innovation, and coordinated policy support. It requires close alignment between energy and water planning, anticipating future constraints, exploiting synergies, and spreading risk. In regions where water is scarce or competition for resources is fierce, adopting wind, solar PV, battery storage, and smart grid integration can safeguard both electricity supply and water security.

In summary: The future of power generation is water-light, flexible, and resilient. By accelerating the adoption of renewables, storage, advanced cooling, process optimization, and digital solutions, the sector can dramatically cut its water footprint, ensure reliable supply, and support wider climate and sustainability goals.

Chapter 2 – Agricultural Water Conservation and Efficiency

Agriculture is the world's largest consumer of freshwater, accounting for nearly 70% of all global withdrawals. From the vast irrigated fields of major breadbasket regions to the smallholder plots sustaining rural communities, the sector's dependence on water is both its greatest strength and most profound vulnerability. As food demand rises in tandem with population growth, and as climate change brings longer droughts, shifting seasons, and unpredictable rainfall, the imperative to conserve water and boost efficiency in agriculture has never been greater.

Traditional agricultural practices, often shaped by local customs, available technologies, and historical water abundance, are increasingly under strain. In many areas, inefficient irrigation methods, over-reliance on water-thirsty crops, and poorly maintained infrastructure result in significant water losses before water even reaches the plants. Inadequate water management not only jeopardizes crop yields and farmer livelihoods, but also intensifies competition with other users and threatens vital ecosystems.

This chapter explores the full spectrum of strategies for agricultural water conservation and efficiency. It begins by examining the sector's diverse water demands and the drivers of inefficiency, considering the complex interplay between crop selection, irrigation technologies, climate factors, and farm management. The chapter then delves into the latest on-farm efficiency technologies, from smart irrigation and soil moisture monitoring to precision scheduling and automated systems that help maximize productivity per drop. System-wide approaches, such as canal lining, conveyance loss reduction, and innovative water pricing, are also highlighted for their potential to achieve larger-scale impacts.

Ultimately, achieving sustainable agricultural water use will require integrated approaches that bridge technical, economic, and behavioral solutions. By adopting new technologies, refining management practices, and incentivizing conservation across the entire agricultural value chain, stakeholders can secure food production while preserving water resources for people and nature alike.

Sectoral Water Demands and Drivers of Inefficiency

Agriculture is by far the largest consumer of freshwater globally, accounting for approximately 70% of total withdrawals. This dominance stems from the inherent water requirements of growing crops and raising livestock, especially in regions dependent on irrigation. As populations rise and dietary preferences shift toward more water-intensive foods, agricultural demand for water is expected to increase further, intensifying pressure on limited supplies and competing uses from cities, industry, and the environment.

At the core of agricultural water use are complex relationships between crop type, irrigation method, local climate, soil conditions, and farm management practices. In many traditional systems, water is diverted from rivers, lakes, or aquifers and applied to fields using open canals or surface irrigation. While such methods can be inexpensive and technically simple, they are often inefficient, with substantial losses due to seepage, evaporation, runoff, and deep percolation. Studies suggest that typical application efficiencies for surface irrigation may range from only 30% to 50%, meaning half or more of the water diverted for agriculture never reaches crops.

Crop selection and irrigation types play a decisive role in shaping water demand. Crops such as rice, sugarcane, and cotton require large volumes of water and are commonly grown in regions facing seasonal or chronic water shortages. High-value horticultural crops, such as fruits and vegetables, may also demand frequent irrigation, but their higher market returns can justify investment in more efficient systems. Conversely, drought-tolerant grains, pulses, and oilseeds can thrive with less water and greater resilience to fluctuating rainfall, making them attractive options for water-scarce areas.

Irrigation methods span a spectrum from traditional surface (furrow, border, basin) to modern pressurized systems like sprinkler and drip irrigation. While surface systems are still prevalent in many countries, particularly for staple crops, the adoption of sprinklers and drip lines has accelerated in regions where water scarcity and high labor costs incentivize efficiency. Drip irrigation, for example, delivers water directly to the root zone, minimizing evaporation and runoff while supporting precise scheduling and nutrient management.

Climate and evapotranspiration challenges further complicate agricultural water management. Hot, dry, and windy conditions can drive up evapotranspiration rates, demanding more frequent and larger irrigation applications to sustain yields. Climate change intensifies these pressures, as more variable rainfall, shifting seasons, and rising temperatures increase both the unpredictability and total volume of irrigation needed. Salinity, exacerbated by poor drainage or over-irrigation, can render water less effective for crops and reduce soil health, further undermining efficiency.

Fragmented land holdings, inadequate extension services, and limited access to finance or technology often hinder farmers' ability to invest in water-saving practices. In some regions, subsidies for water, electricity, or certain crops create perverse incentives, discouraging conservation and reinforcing inefficiency. Traditional water rights systems, designed for an era of abundance, may not adapt quickly enough to evolving scarcity, limiting the effectiveness of collective action for efficiency improvements.

Overall, sectoral inefficiency in agricultural water use is the result of a complex mix of technical, economic, and institutional factors. Addressing these challenges requires a comprehensive approach that combines technology adoption, economic incentives, policy reform, and capacity building. It also demands tailored strategies that reflect the diversity of farming systems, climatic realities, and market conditions found across agricultural regions worldwide.

Crop Selection and Irrigation Types

Choosing the right crop for the local environment is a foundational principle of agricultural water conservation. Crop water requirements vary dramatically, rice grown in paddies needs much more water than wheat or sorghum grown in dryland conditions. In regions where water is limited, shifting to crops with lower water footprints can significantly reduce total agricultural demand without sacrificing income or food security. Crop breeding programs now routinely focus on drought tolerance, heat resistance, and water use efficiency, creating new varieties that can thrive with less irrigation or under irregular rainfall patterns.

The type of irrigation system installed is equally influential. **Surface irrigation**, the most widespread globally, relies on gravity to move water across fields, but suffers from inefficiency due to deep percolation, surface runoff, and uneven distribution. **Sprinkler irrigation** mimics rainfall, allowing for more uniform coverage and reduced labor, but can lose water to evaporation, especially during windy or hot weather. **Drip irrigation** is the gold standard for efficiency, delivering water at low pressure directly to plant roots. Drip systems reduce evaporation, limit weed growth, and facilitate fertigation (applying fertilizer with water), but require upfront investment, reliable maintenance, and regular monitoring to prevent clogging or uneven flow.

The trend toward high-efficiency irrigation is most pronounced in regions facing severe water constraints, but wider adoption is constrained by capital costs, energy needs, and, in some cases, the suitability of existing cropping patterns or farm infrastructure. Governments, donors, and development agencies are increasingly supporting the expansion of efficient irrigation systems through subsidies, technical assistance, and demonstration projects.

Climate and Evapotranspiration Challenges

Weather patterns and microclimates drive water needs on the farm. In areas prone to heatwaves, droughts, or variable rainfall, the challenge is to match irrigation to changing crop requirements while minimizing loss. Technologies such as remote sensing, soil moisture probes, and climate-based scheduling can help farmers tailor their irrigation to actual crop demand, but such tools are not yet universally available or affordable, particularly for smallholders in developing regions.

Evapotranspiration (ET), the combined loss of water from soil evaporation and plant transpiration, is a key metric for efficient water management. ET varies not only with weather but also with crop type, growth stage, soil health, and field management. Optimizing irrigation based on ET forecasts or real-time measurements ensures that crops receive only as much water as needed for maximum growth, reducing waste and runoff.

In summary, the sectoral challenge is clear: agricultural water use is vast, but much of it is lost or poorly allocated due to outdated technologies, suboptimal crop choices, and a lack of precision in management. Overcoming these barriers requires investment in both infrastructure and knowledge, supported by policies that reward conservation and penalize waste.

On-Farm Water Efficiency Technologies

Increasing on-farm water efficiency is essential to closing the gap between water supply and demand in agriculture. Technology is at the heart of this effort, offering both immediate and long-term solutions to improve the productivity of every drop.

Smart Irrigation Systems

Smart irrigation systems integrate sensors, automation, data analytics, and connectivity to optimize the timing, frequency, and quantity of irrigation. These systems leverage real-time data from soil moisture sensors, weather stations, plant stress monitors, and even satellite imagery to inform decisions on when and how much to irrigate.

Automated controllers can adjust irrigation schedules based on local weather forecasts, soil conditions, crop growth stages, and historical data, reducing human error and ensuring water is applied only when truly necessary. Advanced systems may incorporate machine learning algorithms that "learn" optimal patterns for specific fields and conditions, continuously refining recommendations for maximum efficiency and yield.

Benefits of smart irrigation include:

- **Reduced water use**: By avoiding over-irrigation and matching water supply to actual plant needs, savings of 20–50% are routinely reported in pilot projects.
- **Energy and labor savings**: Automation reduces manual monitoring, pumping costs, and the need for workers to operate valves or gates.
- **Improved crop health**: Consistent, precise watering promotes uniform growth and can reduce disease, weed competition, and nutrient leaching.
- **Scalability**: Systems can be tailored for small plots or scaled up for commercial farms, making them adaptable to local context and resources.

Barriers to wider adoption include the initial cost of equipment and installation, the need for technical support and training, and concerns over compatibility with existing infrastructure. Nonetheless, smart irrigation is spreading rapidly in areas where water scarcity is acute, driven by rising water prices, regulatory mandates, and the growing availability of user-friendly, affordable technologies.

Soil Moisture Monitoring and Scheduling

Understanding soil moisture dynamics is fundamental to efficient irrigation. Traditional approaches, such as visual inspection or fixed scheduling, are imprecise and often lead to both under- and over-watering. Modern soil moisture sensors provide real-time data on water content at various depths, allowing for more accurate and dynamic irrigation decisions.

- **Capacitance and TDR sensors**: These measure the dielectric constant of soil, which correlates with moisture content. They provide continuous, automated readings that can be accessed remotely.
- **Tensiometers**: These devices measure soil water tension, indicating how much effort plants must exert to extract water. Tensiometers are particularly useful in sandy soils or for deep-rooted crops.

By combining soil moisture data with weather forecasts and crop growth models, farmers can optimize irrigation intervals and amounts, further reducing waste. Many platforms now provide smartphone apps or web-based dashboards that aggregate data, issue alerts, and offer actionable insights.

Scheduling tools may use simple "checkbook" methods, tracking irrigation and rainfall inputs against known crop needs, or integrate complex algorithms that account for ET rates, root depth, and other variables. This precision ensures water is available when crops need it most and withheld when unnecessary, promoting both yield and resource conservation.

Case applications: Vineyards, orchards, and vegetable farms have been at the forefront of soil moisture technology adoption, as their high-value crops justify investment and benefit markedly from precise water management. Yet, as costs decline and awareness grows, these tools are becoming viable for staple crop production as well.

Challenges: Successful use of soil moisture monitoring requires accurate sensor placement, calibration, and ongoing maintenance. Poorly installed or interpreted sensors can deliver misleading results, underscoring the importance of training and technical support.

In summary: On-farm water efficiency is advancing rapidly through the integration of smart irrigation systems, soil moisture monitoring, and data-driven scheduling. These technologies offer powerful means to align water use with crop demand, enabling farmers to do more with less and build resilience in an era of mounting water constraints.

System-Wide Conservation Approaches

While on-farm technologies deliver substantial gains, broader system-wide interventions are needed to address losses that occur in the conveyance and distribution of water before it even reaches the field, and to create economic incentives that drive efficient use at scale.

Canal Lining and Conveyance Loss Reduction

In many irrigation systems worldwide, water is transported to farms via open canals and ditches, which are prone to significant losses through seepage, evaporation, and leakage. Conveyance losses can account for 30–50% or more of diverted water in poorly maintained or unlined systems. Canal lining, using concrete, plastic membranes, or compacted clay, can dramatically reduce seepage, conserving water for productive use.

- **Concrete lining**: Durable and effective but costly and susceptible to cracking if not properly installed or maintained.
- **Geomembranes**: Flexible, lightweight, and easier to install, making them suitable for remote or temporary applications.
- **Clay lining**: A low-cost alternative where suitable soils are available, though less durable over time.

Beyond lining, regular maintenance, weed control, and modernization of gates and turnouts can also curb losses. The automation of main and lateral canals, using sensors, remote controls, and real-time data, enables operators to match deliveries more closely with crop demand, reducing oversupply and spills.

Pressurized distribution networks (piped systems) further improve delivery efficiency and allow for integration with modern irrigation methods on farms. Although retrofitting traditional systems is capital intensive, the long-term water savings, improved reliability, and ability to expand service justify investment, especially in water-stressed basins.

Institutional arrangements, such as water user associations, play a key role in managing conveyance systems, coordinating maintenance, cost-sharing, and dispute resolution among farmers. Successful examples demonstrate that with strong governance and community engagement, system-wide efficiency can be significantly improved.

Agricultural Water Pricing and Crop Shifts

Economic incentives are powerful drivers of conservation. In many countries, water for agriculture is heavily subsidized or even free, distorting its value and discouraging investment in efficiency. Reforming water pricing to reflect scarcity and delivery costs can encourage farmers to adopt water-saving technologies, shift to less thirsty crops, or intensify production on smaller, more productive areas.

- **Tiered pricing structures**: Charging higher rates for larger volumes incentivizes conservation while protecting smallholder livelihoods.
- **Volumetric pricing**: Metering and billing based on actual use, rather than area or flat fees, is essential for aligning costs with consumption.

- **Tradable water rights**: Allowing farmers to buy and sell water entitlements fosters efficiency and allocates resources to their highest-value uses.

Transitioning to water pricing reform must be managed carefully to avoid negative social impacts, particularly for vulnerable groups. Complementary measures, such as targeted subsidies, access to credit for efficiency upgrades, and extension services, help smooth adjustment and ensure equitable outcomes.

Crop shifting is another key strategy for system-wide water conservation. By promoting or incentivizing the cultivation of drought-resistant varieties, less thirsty cash crops, or mixed farming systems, policymakers can lower the aggregate water footprint of the agricultural sector. Extension programs, demonstration plots, and market support can facilitate these transitions, while research and development expand the range of viable options.

Integrated water resource management approaches, which consider the needs of all sectors and the health of the ecosystem, ensure that conservation gains in agriculture are aligned with broader societal goals. Participatory planning, transparent allocation, and robust monitoring support the sustainable use of water at the basin or watershed scale.

In conclusion, agricultural water conservation and efficiency depend on coordinated action at the crop, farm, and system levels. Progress requires continuous investment in technology, capacity building, policy reform, and institutional strengthening. As the pressures on water resources mount, only a comprehensive and adaptive approach can secure the productivity, sustainability, and resilience of the world's agricultural landscapes.

Chapter 3 – Public Water Supply Efficiency: Urban, Tourism, and Services

Urban areas, tourism hubs, and the broad spectrum of service industries are at the forefront of global water demand. As cities expand, populations grow, and economic activities diversify, the challenge of providing reliable, high-quality water services has become both more complex and urgent. Public water supply systems not only sustain the daily needs of millions but also underpin the functioning of businesses, schools, healthcare facilities, hotels, and recreational sites, forming the backbone of modern economies and vibrant communities.

Yet, these sectors are also characterized by significant inefficiencies and losses. Aging infrastructure, unaccounted-for water from leaks, outdated fixtures, and wasteful behaviors contribute to high levels of non-revenue water and unnecessary strain on finite resources. Meanwhile, the rapid growth of tourism and service industries brings surges in demand, often in regions already facing water scarcity. Hotels, resorts, restaurants, and leisure facilities can have water footprints many times greater than those of local households, heightening the urgency for targeted conservation efforts.

This chapter provides an in-depth exploration of strategies for enhancing water efficiency across urban, tourism, and service sectors. It examines the patterns and drivers of water losses in public supply networks, the specific demands and challenges faced by tourism and service providers, and the suite of technical and behavioral tools available to curb consumption. Emphasis is placed on leak detection, smart metering, greywater reuse, and the adoption of efficient fixtures, alongside the role of incentives, public awareness, and collaborative governance.

By fostering innovation, promoting conservation, and building partnerships among utilities, businesses, and the public, cities and service sectors can transform water management from a hidden cost into a strategic asset. Sustainable public water supply is not only achievable, it is essential for the resilience and prosperity of communities worldwide.

Urban Water Losses and Consumption Patterns

Urban areas are significant consumers of water, with cities accounting for a steadily increasing proportion of global water demand as urbanization intensifies. The pressures on municipal water systems stem from growing populations, expanding infrastructure, rising standards of living, and changes in lifestyle and consumption habits. Managing these demands efficiently is crucial for ensuring water security, supporting economic activity, and protecting environmental quality.

A defining challenge for many urban water utilities is the high level of water loss, often called “non-revenue water”, which includes physical losses from leaks and bursts, as well as commercial losses due to metering inaccuracies or unauthorized consumption. In some developing cities, non-revenue water can exceed 40%, while in the most efficient systems, it may be kept below 10%. Reducing losses is not only a matter of resource conservation but also of financial sustainability for utilities, as lost water represents lost revenue and increased treatment and pumping costs.

Leakage Reduction and Metering

Leakage reduction is typically the first line of defense in improving urban water efficiency. Water distribution networks are often vast, aging, and buried underground, making detection and repair challenging. Over time, pipes corrode, joints fail, and ground movement can cause cracks and breaks. Water loss through leaks is a silent drain on city resources and can go unnoticed for years unless proactive steps are taken.

Modern utilities are investing in a suite of technologies and management practices to tackle leakage. These include:

- **District Metered Areas (DMAs):** Dividing the network into manageable zones allows for precise monitoring and identification of abnormal flows indicative of leaks.
- **Acoustic Sensors and Data Loggers:** These devices "listen" for the sound of escaping water, helping pinpoint the location of leaks before they become catastrophic failures.
- **Pressure Management:** Adjusting system pressure can reduce both the frequency and volume of leaks, extending pipe life and lowering burst rates.
- **Active Leak Detection and Rapid Response Teams:** Continuous surveying, combined with quick repair teams, reduces water losses and minimizes disruption.

Metering is fundamental to both leakage control and overall efficiency. Reliable, accurate meters allow utilities to bill for actual consumption, identify discrepancies, and spot unauthorized use. Smart meters and automated reading technologies are rapidly gaining ground, providing real-time data to both utilities and customers. This enables more dynamic pricing, better detection of anomalies, and the empowerment of consumers to track and manage their own water use.

End-Use Efficiency Measures

Beyond reducing system losses, improving efficiency at the point of consumption is vital. Residential, commercial, and institutional users are responsible for a significant share of urban water demand, and their practices directly shape the city's overall water footprint. End-use efficiency is about delivering the same services, drinking, washing, cleaning, sanitation, cooling, using less water.

Key strategies for end-use efficiency include:

- **Efficient Fixtures and Appliances:** Adoption of low-flow toilets, showerheads, taps, and washing machines can cut household water use by 30–50% without compromising comfort.

- **Behavioral Change Programs:** Education and awareness campaigns encourage residents to adopt water-saving habits such as shorter showers, full loads for washing machines and dishwashers, and shutting off taps while brushing teeth.
- **Submetering in Multi-Unit Buildings:** Installing individual meters for apartments or businesses creates accountability and provides direct incentives for conservation.
- **Commercial Best Practices:** Large water users such as office buildings, malls, and hospitals can implement water audits, upgrade cooling systems, and recycle process water to cut demand.

Urban water conservation is also linked to urban planning and design. Compact development, green infrastructure, permeable surfaces, and integrated stormwater management can all reduce water demand and support more resilient supply systems. Public policies, building codes, and development incentives can drive widespread adoption of efficient technologies and practices across the urban landscape.

In summary, addressing urban water losses and improving end-use efficiency are complementary strategies that together deliver significant water savings, reduce costs, and help cities meet the needs of growing populations without overexploiting local or regional water sources.

Tourism and Service Sector Demands

The tourism and service sectors are major contributors to water demand in many cities and regions, particularly those that serve as global or national tourist destinations. The water footprint of tourism is shaped by accommodation facilities, recreational activities, food and beverage services, and landscaping, often resulting in high per capita consumption compared to local residents.

Tourism's impact on water systems is not just a function of visitor numbers but also of the intensity and patterns of use. Peak tourist seasons may coincide with periods of greatest water scarcity, placing further strain on supply systems and increasing competition with local communities and ecosystems. The service sector, including hotels, restaurants, conference centers, and entertainment venues, relies heavily on reliable, high-quality water supplies for operations and guest satisfaction.

Hotels and Resorts Water Footprint

Hotels and resorts typically have water use profiles far exceeding those of private households, due to amenities such as swimming pools, spas, golf courses, extensive landscaping, frequent laundry services, and high guest turnover. Studies indicate that luxury hotels can consume 400–600 liters of water per guest per day, with even budget accommodations often exceeding 150 liters per guest.

Key areas of water use in hospitality include:

- **Guest Rooms:** Showers, baths, toilets, and sinks account for a large share of in-room water use. Upgrading fixtures and installing flow restrictors can yield immediate savings.
- **Laundry Operations:** High volumes of linens and towels are laundered daily, especially where hotels promote "fresh linens every day" policies. Many establishments are now encouraging guests to reuse towels and linens, reducing wash frequency.
- **Kitchens and Food Services:** Dishwashing, food preparation, and cleaning all require substantial water inputs.
- **Pools, Spas, and Recreation:** Regular refilling, cleaning, and maintenance of pools, spas, and fountains are water-intensive, especially in hot or windy climates.
- **Landscaping:** Ornamental gardens and lawns, especially those with exotic or water-thirsty plant species, can account for up to a third of a hotel's water footprint.

Leading hotels and resorts are adopting comprehensive water management strategies. These include installing high-efficiency fixtures, reusing greywater for irrigation or toilet flushing, adopting towel and linen reuse programs, investing in leak detection, and training staff in water-efficient practices. Many are also benchmarking their water use against industry standards and seeking certification through programs such as LEED, Green Key, or EarthCheck.

Food Services and Landscaping Practices

Restaurants, cafes, bars, and catering services are integral to both tourism and local economies. Their water use is concentrated in dishwashing, food preparation, cleaning, and restrooms. High customer turnover, large-scale catering events, and 24/7 operations in tourist hotspots can further elevate demand.

Best practices for water conservation in food services include:

- **Low-Flow Pre-Rinse Spray Valves:** These can cut dishwashing water use by half.
- **Efficient Dishwashers and Steamers:** Upgrading to Energy Star-rated appliances saves water and energy.
- **Smart Kitchen Practices:** Thawing food in refrigerators instead of under running water, batch washing dishes, and using basins for vegetable rinsing reduce waste.
- **Restroom Retrofits:** Installing dual-flush toilets, sensor-activated faucets, and waterless urinals in customer and staff restrooms.

Outdoor landscaping is another major water consumer in the service sector. Hotels, resorts, restaurants, and malls often feature extensive lawns, gardens, and decorative water features to create attractive environments for guests and customers. Yet, traditional landscaping practices, such as daily watering of lawns and the use of non-native, high-water plants, can be highly inefficient.

Water-smart landscaping ("xeriscaping") offers a solution by emphasizing:

- **Native and Drought-Tolerant Species:** Plants adapted to the local climate require less irrigation and are more resilient to drought.
- **Soil Improvement and Mulching:** Enhances water retention and reduces evaporation.
- **Efficient Irrigation Systems:** Drip irrigation and smart controllers ensure water is delivered precisely when and where it is needed.
- **Rainwater Harvesting:** Capturing and using rainwater for landscape irrigation reduces reliance on potable supplies.

By combining best practices in kitchen operations, guest services, and landscaping, the tourism and service sectors can substantially reduce their water footprints while enhancing operational efficiency, cost savings, and reputation among environmentally conscious travelers.

Tools for Conservation in Urban and Tourist Areas

Delivering water efficiency at scale in cities and tourist destinations requires a comprehensive set of tools and interventions that combine technical, economic, and behavioral approaches. Utilities, city governments, and businesses have developed a diverse portfolio of conservation strategies tailored to local conditions and user profiles.

Incentives and Public Awareness Campaigns

Incentives are among the most effective tools for driving the uptake of water-saving technologies and practices. Utilities and governments may offer:

- **Rebates and Subsidies:** For installing low-flow fixtures, high-efficiency appliances, rainwater harvesting systems, or greywater recycling units.
- **Retrofit Programs:** Direct installation or replacement of inefficient devices in residential and commercial buildings, often targeting high-use neighborhoods or sectors.

- **Tiered Pricing Structures:** Charging higher rates for larger water users encourages conservation while protecting basic needs for low-income or vulnerable groups.
- **Grant Programs:** Funding for community-led initiatives, research, or pilot projects in water conservation.

Public awareness campaigns are crucial for fostering behavioral change and building a culture of conservation. Successful campaigns:

- **Engage Diverse Audiences:** Tailor messages for schools, businesses, homeowners, tourists, and marginalized groups.
- **Use Multiple Channels:** TV, radio, social media, billboards, community events, and partnerships with influencers or local leaders.
- **Demonstrate Impact:** Share success stories, data on water savings, and testimonials from early adopters.
- **Promote Water "Champions":** Recognize individuals, businesses, or neighborhoods that have achieved significant savings.

Behavioral nudges, such as comparative water use reports ("you use 20% more water than your neighbors"), gamified conservation challenges, or public commitments, can be powerful motivators for sustained change.

Greywater Reuse and Fixture Upgrades

Greywater, lightly used water from sinks, showers, baths, and laundry, represents a major opportunity for water recycling in urban and tourist settings. While not suitable for drinking, greywater can be safely reused for toilet flushing, landscape irrigation, or even cooling towers with appropriate treatment.

Best practices in greywater reuse include:

- **Onsite Collection and Treatment:** Simple systems collect greywater separately from blackwater (sewage), filter it, and store it for non-potable uses.
- **Code and Regulatory Support:** Clear guidelines and standards ensure safety and public health, and support wider adoption.
- **Integration with Building Design:** New buildings can be "pre-plumbed" for greywater separation, making future retrofits easier and less expensive.
- **Community-Scale Systems:** In high-density or multi-unit settings, shared greywater treatment and reuse infrastructure can achieve economies of scale.

Fixture upgrades are the backbone of water efficiency at the end-use level. Advances in design and technology have made it possible to deliver the same level of service with dramatically less water.

- **Ultra-Low-Flow Toilets:** Use 4.8 liters or less per flush, compared to older models that use 13–20 liters.
- **High-Efficiency Showerheads:** Deliver strong flow at less than 7.5 liters per minute.
- **Sensor Faucets and Aerators:** Automatically shut off when not in use and mix air into water to maintain pressure while reducing flow.

Cities and utilities may mandate fixture standards through building codes, offer free or discounted upgrades, or require replacements during property sales or renovations.

Bringing It All Together: Integrated Approaches

The most successful urban and tourist water conservation programs take an integrated approach, combining incentives, education, regulation, technology, and infrastructure investments. Key ingredients for success include:

- **Strong Institutional Leadership:** Committed utilities, city governments, and business leaders can set ambitious targets, track progress, and drive innovation.
- **Data-Driven Decision Making:** Smart meters, water audits, and performance dashboards enable continuous improvement and accountability.
- **Collaboration and Partnerships:** Engagement with NGOs, community groups, industry associations, and the private sector broadens reach and amplifies impact.
- **Equity and Inclusion:** Ensuring that all residents, businesses, and visitors have access to conservation resources and are not disproportionately burdened by pricing or policy changes.

In conclusion, water efficiency in public supply, tourism, and services is a multi-faceted challenge requiring both systemic and targeted solutions. By combining leakage reduction, end-use efficiency, sector-specific strategies, and a comprehensive toolkit for conservation, cities and businesses can secure resilient, sustainable water supplies for present and future generations.

Chapter 4 – Industrial Water Use and Circular Water Practices

Industry stands as one of the most influential, and often underestimated, players in global water consumption. From power generation and manufacturing to food processing, textiles, and chemicals, industrial activities collectively account for a significant share of total water withdrawals, particularly in advanced and rapidly developing economies. Water is integral to virtually every stage of production, used for cooling, washing, dissolving, transporting, and transforming materials. However, the sector's reliance on water also exposes it to risks: operational disruptions, regulatory pressures, rising costs, and growing scrutiny from consumers and stakeholders concerned with sustainability.

As concerns over water scarcity and pollution intensify, industries are increasingly compelled to rethink traditional "take-make-dispose" models. The circular economy paradigm offers a transformative path forward, one that prioritizes resource efficiency, closed-loop systems, and the recovery and reuse of water within and between facilities. Embracing circular water practices enables businesses to reduce fresh water intake, minimize wastewater generation, and build resilience against volatile supply and environmental regulations.

This chapter explores the evolving landscape of industrial water use, focusing on the drivers of demand, patterns of consumption, and sources of inefficiency across major sectors. It highlights the latest advances in process optimization, automation, leak detection, and smart monitoring, technologies that empower operators to identify and address inefficiencies in real time. The chapter also examines the emergence of industrial symbiosis, where neighboring companies collaborate to share water resources, exchange by-products, and co-manage treatment infrastructure for mutual benefit.

By integrating circular principles into their operations, industries can not only reduce costs and environmental impacts but also strengthen competitiveness and corporate reputation. Ultimately, a shift toward circular water management is central to both the sustainability of industry and the broader goal of ensuring water security for all sectors of society.

Industrial Sectoral Demands and Water Uses

The industrial sector is a significant and often overlooked user of freshwater resources worldwide. Industrial water use accounts for approximately 20% of global freshwater withdrawals, but in high-income and heavily industrialized economies, this share can rise to over 50%. The sheer scale and diversity of industry mean that water is used in a multitude of processes, from cooling and heating to washing, dissolving, transporting, and chemical transformation. Efficient management of water in industry is crucial not only for operational reliability and cost control but also for environmental stewardship and compliance with increasingly strict regulations.

High-Use Industries and Process Water Needs

Industrial water use is not uniform; certain sectors stand out as especially intensive users. The most water-demanding industries include:

- **Thermoelectric power generation**: Requires vast quantities for cooling purposes, as described in Chapter 1.
- **Pulp and paper manufacturing**: Water is used extensively in pulping, washing, bleaching, and paper production. A single ton of paper can require tens of thousands of liters of water, depending on technology and recycling rates.
- **Food and beverage processing**: Water is essential for cleaning, cooking, sterilizing, conveying raw materials, and as an ingredient in products themselves.
- **Textile and dyeing**: Large amounts of water are required for washing, dyeing, rinsing, and finishing fibers and fabrics.

- **Chemical and petrochemical industries**: Use water as both a reactant and a solvent, and for cooling, product washing, and emissions control.
- **Metals and mining**: Water is used in ore processing, flotation, dust suppression, cooling, and equipment washing.
- **Electronics and semiconductor manufacturing**: Requires ultra-pure water for wafer production, cleaning, and rinsing, with strict control over impurities.

Water requirements are determined by process type, product output, plant size, equipment efficiency, and, increasingly, the regulatory and environmental context. In addition to direct process water needs, industries must consider water for facility maintenance, landscaping, sanitation, and fire protection.

Mapping Water Flows and Losses

A critical first step in industrial water management is mapping water flows throughout the facility or process chain. Water flow mapping, or water auditing, provides a comprehensive understanding of where, how, and why water is used, and where it is lost or wasted. This involves:

- **Inventorying all water inputs**: Sourcing from municipal supply, groundwater, surface water, or reclaimed sources.
- **Charting process flows**: Tracking water through each production stage, identifying transfer points, storage, and treatment steps.
- **Identifying points of loss**: These include leaks, overflows, inefficient equipment, and unmonitored discharges.
- **Measuring outputs**: Monitoring water that exits the facility as product content, steam, emissions, treated effluent, or waste.

Data collection tools range from simple manual meter readings to sophisticated, real-time monitoring systems using flow meters, sensors, and data loggers. Comprehensive mapping uncovers "hidden" losses, such as small, continuous leaks, inefficient cleaning practices, or excessive blowdown in boilers and cooling towers, that can add up to substantial volumes over time.

Water flow mapping also helps quantify the "water footprint" of products and processes, which is increasingly required for sustainability reporting and supply chain transparency. This information is foundational for benchmarking performance, setting reduction targets, and prioritizing investments in efficiency and reuse.

Inefficiency in industrial water use often results from outdated equipment, poor maintenance, lack of automation, or low awareness among staff. In some regions, artificially low water prices and weak enforcement of discharge standards create little incentive for conservation. However, as water scarcity increases and costs rise, through tariffs, treatment fees, or compliance penalties, industries are being driven to invest in smarter, more sustainable water management practices.

Improving Water Efficiency in Operations

Improving operational water efficiency is a multifaceted endeavor that involves both technological upgrades and better management practices. Efficient use of water reduces operational costs, ensures compliance, and supports broader corporate sustainability goals.

Process Optimization and Automation

Process optimization focuses on minimizing water use without compromising product quality or output. Key strategies include:

- **Process redesign**: Modifying production steps to use less water, such as switching from wet to dry processes, reconfiguring cleaning protocols, or optimizing batch sizes.

- **Water-saving equipment**: Installing high-efficiency washers, spray nozzles, closed-circuit cooling systems, and counter-current rinsing tanks that maximize use of each drop.
- **Reuse and cascade use**: Allowing water from one stage (e.g., initial washing) to be reused for less critical stages (e.g., pre-washing or flushing), minimizing freshwater intake.
- **Reducing overflows and oversprays**: Installing controls or flow restrictors to prevent water from running unnecessarily during cleaning or rinsing operations.

Automation is a critical enabler of water efficiency, providing precise control, monitoring, and adjustment of water use in real time. The deployment of programmable logic controllers (PLCs), SCADA systems, and Internet of Things (IoT) sensors enables:

- **Real-time monitoring**: Instant feedback on flow rates, pressure, temperature, and water quality at key points in the system.
- **Automatic shutoff and flow control**: Water use is automatically reduced or stopped during equipment downtime or non-production periods.
- **Data analytics**: Historical and live data are used to identify inefficiencies, optimize process scheduling, and predict future water needs.

For example, in food processing plants, sensors can detect when conveyors or washers are empty and automatically shut off sprays, preventing unnecessary use. In textile factories, automated dosing and rinsing systems deliver only the amount of water needed for each dye lot, reducing both water and chemical consumption.

Process optimization and automation require initial investment in equipment, integration, and staff training, but the return on investment is often rapid, particularly where water costs or compliance pressures are high.

Maintenance and Leak Detection

Regular maintenance is fundamental to operational efficiency. Industrial facilities are complex environments where valves, joints, pipes, tanks, and pumps are under constant stress from pressure, temperature changes, and vibration. Over time, this leads to wear, corrosion, and eventual failure, resulting in leaks, spills, and water loss.

Effective leak detection and maintenance programs include:

- **Routine inspections**: Scheduled walkthroughs and inspections using visual checks, moisture sensors, and acoustic devices.
- **Predictive maintenance**: Using sensor data to anticipate when components are likely to fail, allowing for planned repairs rather than reactive fixes.
- **Automated alerts**: Sensors trigger alarms or shut down equipment when abnormal water flows, pressures, or tank levels are detected.
- **Staff training**: Ensuring that maintenance teams and operators recognize the signs of leaks and understand the importance of prompt repairs.

Leak detection is especially critical in industries with large, complex piping networks, such as chemicals, petrochemicals, and food processing, where even small leaks can be difficult to spot and costly over time. Thermal imaging, ultrasonic devices, and tracer dyes are increasingly used to pinpoint hard-to-detect leaks.

Effective maintenance extends the lifespan of equipment, reduces unplanned downtime, and minimizes the risk of regulatory non-compliance due to excessive discharge or environmental contamination. As water becomes more valuable and regulation more stringent, proactive maintenance is no longer optional but a core business imperative.

In summary, improving water efficiency in industrial operations requires a dual focus on process optimization and robust maintenance. The integration of automation and digital tools is accelerating progress, making it easier to manage water use precisely, detect losses early, and drive continuous improvement across facilities.

Recycling, Reuse, and Industrial Symbiosis

The adoption of recycling, reuse, and symbiotic practices in industry is transforming water management from a linear "take-make-dispose" model to a circular, resource-smart approach. This shift is driven by water scarcity, rising costs, environmental regulations, and the pursuit of sustainability targets. Moving toward circular water use not only cuts demand for freshwater but can also create new business opportunities and strengthen relationships with local communities and stakeholders.

Closed-Loop and Cascading Systems

A closed-loop water system is designed to retain and recirculate water within a facility, minimizing the intake of fresh water and the discharge of wastewater. Water is captured after use, treated to remove contaminants, and then fed back into the same or different processes. The level of treatment required depends on the intended reuse, high-purity processes require advanced filtration, while cooling or washing may need only basic treatment.

Key elements of closed-loop systems:

- **Segregation of streams**: Separating high- and low-contamination wastewater at the source enables tailored treatment and maximizes reuse potential.
- **On-site treatment plants**: Facilities install their own filtration, sedimentation, chemical, or biological treatment units to process water for reuse.
- **Continuous monitoring**: Real-time tracking of water quality, flow rates, and system integrity ensures that reused water meets process requirements and regulatory standards.

- **Integration with process controls**: Automated systems adjust flows and treatment rates dynamically, adapting to production schedules and quality needs.

Closed-loop systems are common in industries such as electronics, automotive, steel, and pulp and paper, where large volumes of water are used and regulatory pressures on discharge are high. Benefits include reduced water bills, lower effluent treatment costs, enhanced compliance, and improved resilience during droughts or water restrictions.

Cascading systems are a variation on the closed-loop approach, where water is reused sequentially in processes with descending water quality requirements. For example, in a beverage bottling plant, water used for bottle rinsing can be captured and reused for floor washing or cooling. In a textile plant, rinse water from a high-quality dyeing process may be used for pre-washing or cleaning.

These approaches optimize the use of each liter of water, extracting maximum value before final discharge or disposal. They also reduce the pollutant load in effluent streams, easing the burden on municipal or regional wastewater treatment infrastructure.

Challenges and considerations:

- Initial capital investment in treatment and monitoring technology can be significant, but is typically offset by long-term savings.
- System design must account for potential fouling, scaling, or accumulation of trace contaminants.
- Worker training and process controls are essential to ensure consistent performance and product quality.

Water Exchange in Industrial Clusters

Industrial symbiosis refers to the sharing of resources, including water, between different companies or facilities in close geographic proximity. In industrial clusters, one plant's waste or by-product becomes another's resource. Water exchange arrangements can provide mutual benefits by reducing each participant's need for fresh water, lowering treatment costs, and improving the local water balance.

Models of water exchange:

- **Direct reuse**: Treated effluent from one factory (such as a food processor or beverage plant) is supplied via pipeline to a neighboring facility (such as a power station or chemical plant) for use in cooling, washing, or process operations.
- **Shared treatment facilities**: Multiple industries collaborate to build and operate a central treatment plant that recycles water for use by all participants, achieving economies of scale and technical efficiency.
- **Rainwater and stormwater harvesting**: Clusters may jointly invest in the collection and storage of rainwater or stormwater, using it to supplement process water or for non-potable uses across the site.

Case examples:

- In some industrial parks, petrochemical and steel manufacturers exchange steam condensate, cooling water, or treated wastewater.
- Eco-industrial parks in Europe and Asia have successfully implemented water networks linking several companies, reducing aggregate withdrawals and discharges.

Water exchange is facilitated by spatial proximity, complementary water quality needs, and strong governance arrangements. It requires investment in infrastructure, monitoring, and contractual agreements to ensure fair allocation, cost-sharing, and compliance with regulations.

Benefits of industrial symbiosis include:

- Enhanced resource efficiency and cost savings for all participants.
- Improved environmental performance, with lower cumulative impacts on local water bodies.
- Strengthened resilience to drought or supply restrictions through shared storage and backup systems.
- Positive reputational and regulatory outcomes from innovative, collaborative approaches.

Barriers include:

- Coordination and trust among companies with differing priorities or corporate cultures.
- Legal and liability concerns related to water quality, system failures, or cross-contamination.
- The need for supportive policy frameworks, planning incentives, and technical assistance from local authorities or development agencies.

The Circular Future of Industrial Water Use

The growing adoption of circular water practices marks a paradigm shift for industry. Companies are increasingly moving beyond compliance-driven approaches to proactive stewardship, viewing water not just as a cost or risk, but as a core component of competitiveness, innovation, and corporate responsibility.

Key drivers of this transition include:

- **Scarcity and risk**: Water is recognized as a strategic risk to business continuity, with supply disruptions or pollution incidents threatening operations, profits, and reputation.
- **Regulation and reporting**: Environmental standards, disclosure requirements, and investor expectations push companies to reduce withdrawals, discharges, and water footprints.

- **Economics**: Rising water costs, treatment fees, and potential fines for non-compliance create powerful incentives for efficiency and reuse.
- **Technology**: Advances in treatment, monitoring, automation, and digitalization lower barriers and increase returns on investment in circular systems.
- **Stakeholder expectations**: Customers, communities, and NGOs expect industry to "do more with less" and play a leading role in protecting shared water resources.

In conclusion, industrial water use is being transformed by the twin forces of efficiency and circularity. By optimizing operations, maintaining robust infrastructure, and embracing recycling, reuse, and symbiotic practices, industries can reduce their water footprints, cut costs, and strengthen resilience. These efforts not only benefit individual companies, but contribute to the sustainability and well-being of entire regions, demonstrating that water-smart industry is integral to a sustainable future.

Chapter 5 – Mining, Quarrying, and Construction Sector Water Management

Mining, quarrying, and construction are pillars of economic development, providing the raw materials and infrastructure essential for modern societies. Yet these sectors are also among the most intensive users of water, with wide-ranging impacts on local hydrology, water quality, and the communities and ecosystems that depend on shared resources. The extraction of minerals, aggregates, and building materials demands significant volumes of water for drilling, dust suppression, ore and aggregate processing, concrete production, and site maintenance. In many regions, these activities occur in water-scarce environments, increasing the urgency for smarter and more responsible water management.

Historically, the mining, quarrying, and construction industries have faced criticism for their water use, pollution, and legacy of environmental degradation. Uncontrolled discharges, inefficient processing, and lack of proper planning have resulted in contaminated waterways, declining groundwater levels, and social conflict. Today, however, mounting regulatory pressures, heightened community expectations, and the physical risks of water scarcity are driving a new era of innovation and accountability.

This chapter provides a comprehensive overview of water management strategies tailored to the unique challenges of extraction and construction. It examines sectoral water demands and critical uses, from drilling and dewatering to concrete batching and aggregate washing, while exploring the latest technologies and practices for boosting efficiency. Particular emphasis is placed on dry processing, real-time monitoring, adaptive operations, and the integration of on-site water recycling and recovery systems. The chapter also discusses the role of rainwater harvesting, treatment of tailings, and the adoption of zero liquid discharge approaches as part of a broader move toward sustainability.

Water Use in Resource Extraction and Processing

Mining, quarrying, and construction sectors are crucial drivers of economic development, infrastructure, and industrial growth across the globe. Yet, they are also substantial users of water resources, with specific processes requiring large volumes of water for extraction, material processing, site management, and dust suppression. The management of water in these sectors is often complicated by site-specific conditions, environmental risks, regulatory scrutiny, and the need to balance operational efficiency with community and ecological concerns.

Drilling, Dust Suppression, and Dewatering

The extraction of minerals, aggregates, and other resources from the earth is inherently water-intensive. **Drilling**, the initial phase of mining and quarrying, requires water for lubricating drill bits, cooling equipment, and managing cuttings. Depending on geological conditions and the depth or type of mineral targeted, drilling water demand can range from modest to substantial. Water-based drilling fluids, or "muds," help maintain borehole stability, transport cuttings to the surface, and control subsurface pressures. In some operations, air drilling or foam may substitute for water, but these methods are not always feasible or effective.

Dust suppression is a major operational and environmental concern in mining, quarrying, and large-scale construction. The disturbance of soils, rocks, and aggregates releases fine particles into the air, posing health risks to workers and surrounding communities, reducing visibility, and potentially violating air quality standards. Water is the most common dust control agent, applied through sprinklers, misters, water trucks, or fixed sprays on haul roads, crushers, and conveyor belts. Effective dust control can require thousands of liters per day on large sites, especially in arid climates or during dry seasons.

Dewatering is the process of removing water from excavations, tunnels, open pits, or underground mines. Groundwater inflow, rainfall, and process water can accumulate in active mining or construction areas, hindering operations and threatening equipment or worker safety. Dewatering systems use pumps, drains, sumps, and sometimes wells or tunnels to manage water levels. The extracted water may be treated for reuse on-site, discharged to the environment, or sent to municipal or industrial treatment plants. Dewatering can also alter local hydrology, lowering groundwater tables and affecting surrounding ecosystems or water users, a risk that requires careful monitoring and mitigation.

In sum, drilling, dust suppression, and dewatering represent foundational water uses in resource extraction. Efficient management of these activities is vital for operational continuity, regulatory compliance, and environmental protection.

Concrete and Aggregate Water Demand

The construction sector, particularly in urbanizing and rapidly developing regions, is a voracious user of water for concrete and aggregate production. **Concrete**, the world's most widely used building material, is made by mixing cement, sand, gravel (or crushed stone), and water. Water is essential for initiating the chemical reactions (hydration) that harden cement and give concrete its strength and durability. The water-to-cement ratio is a critical quality parameter, affecting both workability and final performance.

The production of ready-mix concrete, precast elements, mortars, and cement-based grouts involves large volumes of water, not only in the mix but also for washing equipment, curing finished products, and controlling dust in storage and handling of aggregates. Recycling water within batching plants is increasingly common, but the baseline demand remains high.

Aggregate processing, crushing, screening, washing, also uses water for dust control, cleaning raw materials, and separating fines from usable sand or gravel. Some operations rely on simple wet screening, while others incorporate advanced washing plants or settling ponds to manage fine particles and recover reusable water.

The environmental and operational impacts of concrete and aggregate water use are magnified by the scale and intensity of construction activity. Localized water scarcity, pollution from wastewater discharge, and competition with municipal or agricultural users are common concerns, especially near urban centers or in water-stressed basins.

Construction activities, such as earthworks, road building, tunneling, and site preparation, further contribute to water demand for dust control, compaction, hydro-demolition, cleaning, and landscaping. Seasonal or episodic demands (e.g., large pours, accelerated schedules, hot-weather concreting) can create spikes in water use that challenge both site management and local supplies.

Managing water use in concrete and aggregate operations requires close attention to mix design, process efficiency, material handling, and opportunities for recycling or substitution. As sustainability becomes a key priority in the construction industry, clients and contractors are increasingly seeking ways to reduce the water footprint of building projects through innovation, certification, and integrated planning.

Efficiency Gains Through Technology and Planning

The drive for greater efficiency in mining, quarrying, and construction is propelled by escalating water costs, tighter regulation, public scrutiny, and the imperative to maintain a social license to operate. Advancements in technology and smarter planning are enabling significant reductions in water demand, while maintaining or improving operational performance.

Dry Processing and Efficient Separation

One of the most impactful strategies for reducing water use in extraction and material processing is the shift from wet to dry methods. **Dry processing** techniques eliminate or greatly reduce the need for water in separation, screening, and beneficiation of ores or aggregates.

In mining, technologies such as **dry crushing, screening, and air classification** are being adopted in place of traditional wet separation or washing. For example, high-frequency vibrating screens and advanced air classifiers can efficiently separate mineral particles without water, producing high-quality products suitable for further processing or sale.

Magnetic and electrostatic separation are also dry methods that can concentrate ores or remove impurities from minerals, reducing the water demand associated with flotation or gravity concentration. In some cases, these approaches can enable processing of low-grade ores that would otherwise be uneconomic or environmentally damaging using conventional water-intensive methods.

In aggregate production, dry processing can involve the use of dust collectors, baghouses, and covered conveyors to minimize airborne dust and reduce the reliance on water sprays for dust control. Dry crushing and screening reduce the need for washing, and improvements in material handling can limit spillage and waste.

For construction projects, **soil stabilization and dust control** can be achieved through chemical suppressants, polymer additives, or mechanical compaction, reducing or eliminating the need for water-based methods. Technologies such as hydrodemolition robots use precisely controlled jets of water to remove concrete with minimal overall consumption compared to manual washing or high-volume flushing.

Adopting dry processing often requires upfront investment in equipment and training, but the benefits include lower water costs, reduced wastewater generation, and a smaller environmental footprint. Dry methods are especially valuable in arid regions or where access to water is limited, expensive, or contested.

Real-Time Monitoring and Adaptive Operations

Advances in digital technologies and automation are revolutionizing water management in extraction and construction. **Real-time monitoring** enables operators to track water use, detect leaks or inefficiencies, and respond rapidly to changing conditions.

Modern mines and quarries use **remote sensing, flow meters, water level sensors, and automated controls** to manage dewatering pumps, optimize dust suppression schedules, and track water quality across the site. Centralized dashboards aggregate data from across the operation, providing a comprehensive view of water inputs, outputs, losses, and recycling rates.

Adaptive operations leverage this data to adjust water management strategies dynamically. For example:

- **Dust suppression systems** can be linked to weather forecasts, turning on only when wind speeds, humidity, or temperature exceed threshold values.
- **Dewatering pumps** can be automated to operate at optimal efficiency, reducing energy and water wastage.
- **Batching and concrete mixing plants** can calibrate water addition in real time based on temperature, humidity, and moisture content of aggregates.

Predictive analytics can anticipate spikes in water demand or identify emerging problems, such as blocked pipes, failing seals, or unusually high consumption rates. Maintenance can be scheduled proactively, reducing downtime and preventing costly failures.

Mobile apps and cloud-based platforms allow field teams to record water use, inspect equipment, and report incidents directly from the worksite, improving coordination and accountability. In construction, Building Information Modeling (BIM) can incorporate water use scenarios into project planning, identifying opportunities for efficiency and risk reduction before construction begins.

Overall, technology-enabled monitoring and adaptive operations are key to driving water efficiency, reducing waste, and ensuring compliance with environmental standards. They empower operators to make informed decisions, allocate resources effectively, and demonstrate responsible water stewardship to regulators, investors, and communities.

On-Site Water Recycling and Recovery

While reducing baseline water use is crucial, the ability to recycle and recover water on-site provides a powerful additional tool for conservation, especially in water-scarce regions or for operations with high process water demand.

Rainwater and Wastewater Reuse

Rainwater harvesting offers a relatively simple and low-cost way to supplement process water supply in mining, quarrying, and construction. By capturing runoff from roofs, paved areas, or stockpiles, operators can store rainwater in tanks or ponds for use in dust suppression, equipment washing, or even in concrete production. This reduces the need to draw on municipal or surface water sources, especially during wet seasons or in areas with high rainfall variability.

On-site wastewater reuse involves collecting, treating, and recycling water from process streams, wash-down, dewatering, and site drainage. Treatment technologies may include sedimentation, filtration, clarification, and sometimes advanced methods such as membrane filtration or chemical dosing, depending on the intended reuse.

For example, water used in washing aggregates or cleaning equipment can be routed to settling ponds where solids settle out and water is recovered for reuse. In underground mines or tunneling, dewatering water can be treated and cycled back for dust control or drilling.

On large construction projects, water from curing concrete, cleaning vehicles, or controlling dust can be collected, filtered, and reused multiple times before final disposal. Some innovative contractors set up closed-loop systems, moving water between site activities to maximize utility and minimize discharge.

Rainwater and wastewater reuse systems require careful design to prevent contamination, clogging, or water quality issues that could impact product performance or environmental compliance. Regular monitoring and maintenance are essential to ensure safety and effectiveness.

Treatment of Tailings and Process Water

Tailings, the waste materials left after extracting valuable minerals, are one of the biggest water management challenges in mining. Tailings are typically stored in large ponds or impoundments, where water slowly evaporates or seeps away. However, new approaches are enabling significant recovery and reuse of water from tailings streams.

Thickened tailings technology involves removing more water from tailings before storage, producing a dense slurry that reduces seepage, accelerates drying, and enables greater water recovery for return to the process plant. **Paste backfill**, where thickened tailings are mixed with cement and pumped back into underground voids, both stabilizes the mine and returns water to the cycle.

Filtration and dewatering technologies, such as vacuum filters, belt presses, and centrifuges, can extract additional water from tailings or sludge, producing drier waste and cleaner process water for reuse. These technologies are increasingly being mandated by regulators seeking to minimize environmental risks from tailings dams.

In aggregate and concrete production, **recycling wash water** is becoming standard practice. Settling basins and clarifiers separate solids, enabling reuse of water for subsequent batches or cleaning cycles. Sludge or recovered fines can be incorporated into low-grade construction materials or disposed of responsibly.

Zero liquid discharge (ZLD) systems are an emerging best practice in high-risk or high-value operations. ZLD combines multiple treatment steps, evaporation, crystallization, filtration, to ensure that no wastewater leaves the site. All water is either recycled or converted to solid waste for safe disposal. While capital-intensive, ZLD delivers maximum water recovery, environmental protection, and regulatory certainty.

Benefits of on-site recycling and recovery include:

- Substantially reduced freshwater demand and operational costs.
- Enhanced compliance with discharge limits and environmental permits.
- Increased operational resilience during droughts or water restrictions.
- Improved community relations and reduced conflicts with other water users.

Challenges include:

- Investment in infrastructure, monitoring, and maintenance.
- Management of accumulated contaminants, salinity, or scaling in recycled water streams.
- Regulatory approval and oversight, particularly for innovative or large-scale recycling systems.

Chapter 6 – Integrated Monitoring and Performance Metrics

In the drive for sustainable water management, what gets measured truly gets managed. Integrated monitoring and performance metrics form the backbone of modern water conservation and efficiency strategies, enabling organizations, utilities, and policymakers to move beyond guesswork and anecdote toward data-driven decision-making. As the complexity and scale of water challenges grow, spanning sectors, jurisdictions, and climates, the ability to accurately track water use, identify inefficiencies, benchmark performance, and verify progress has never been more critical.

Traditionally, water management relied on periodic, manual measurements and retrospective assessments that provided only a fragmented view of system performance. Today, technological advancements have revolutionized the landscape. The integration of real-time sensors, remote metering, SCADA systems, and digital analytics empowers managers to gain a granular, continuous picture of water flows, losses, and opportunities for intervention. These tools not only drive operational efficiency but also support transparency, accountability, and continuous improvement.

This chapter delves into the foundational elements of integrated monitoring and performance metrics. It examines the role of water audits and key performance indicators (KPIs) in diagnosing and prioritizing areas for action. Benchmarking against industry standards and best practices helps organizations set ambitious yet achievable goals. The chapter also explores the transformative power of digitalization, how the deployment of IoT sensors, advanced analytics, and real-time feedback systems enables rapid detection of leaks, automated adjustments, and smarter resource allocation.

Finally, the chapter highlights the importance of robust reporting and verification systems, including sustainability certifications and public disclosure. These elements foster stakeholder trust and provide the basis for informed investment and policy decisions.

By embracing integrated monitoring and robust performance metrics, all sectors can ensure that water conservation efforts are targeted, effective, and aligned with broader sustainability and resilience objectives.

Measuring Water Use and Efficiency

Effective water conservation and efficiency strategies depend on accurate measurement, analysis, and continuous improvement. The first step in this process is understanding how much water is being used, where it is used, and how efficiently it is converted into value, whether that value is energy, agricultural output, manufactured goods, or essential services. Integrated monitoring and performance metrics transform water management from a reactive, compliance-driven exercise to a proactive and strategic function, supporting sustainability, resilience, and long-term cost savings.

Measuring water use begins with establishing a comprehensive water balance for each facility, system, or region. This includes all sources (such as surface water, groundwater, rainwater, and recycled water), all points of use (processes, cooling, cleaning, irrigation, domestic), and all outputs (product content, evaporation, discharge, and losses). Only with a complete understanding of inflows and outflows can organizations identify opportunities for efficiency, target areas for intervention, and set meaningful goals.

Water Audits and Key Performance Indicators

Water audits are systematic examinations of water use within a facility, operation, or supply network. These audits can be simple, one-off assessments or complex, recurring reviews integrated into management systems. The process typically involves:

- Mapping all water inputs, uses, and outputs.
- Quantifying losses due to leaks, overflows, or inefficiency.
- Evaluating water quality at various stages and for different uses.
- Identifying "hidden" consumption, such as auxiliary systems, equipment cooling, or maintenance.
- Recommending prioritized actions for improvement based on costs, benefits, and feasibility.

Water audits may be conducted internally or by third-party specialists, and are increasingly required by regulations, industry standards, or certification programs. The results inform investment decisions, operational changes, and compliance reporting.

KPIs for water management transform audit data into actionable metrics. KPIs are tailored to the context, what is meaningful for a municipal utility may differ from an industrial plant, farm, or resort. Common water KPIs include:

- **Water use per unit output:** For example, liters per kilowatt-hour, per ton of product, per guest-night, or per hectare.
- **Water loss percentage:** The ratio of non-revenue or unaccounted-for water to total supply.
- **Water recycling/reuse ratio:** The proportion of total water demand met through recycled or reclaimed sources.
- **Water efficiency improvement rate:** Year-on-year change in water intensity.
- **Compliance rates:** Adherence to discharge, withdrawal, or reuse permits.

KPIs must be relevant, reliable, and repeatable. They should provide both management and frontline staff with clear signals about performance, priorities, and progress toward strategic objectives. Where possible, KPIs are benchmarked against industry norms, best practices, or regulatory standards.

Benchmarking and Best Practice Identification

Benchmarking is the process of comparing water performance metrics against peers, industry standards, or global leaders. This allows organizations to:

- Understand their position relative to similar operations or competitors.
- Set realistic, data-driven improvement targets.
- Identify "best-in-class" approaches, technologies, and practices that drive superior results.
- Motivate continuous improvement and innovation by making performance visible and comparable.

Benchmarking can occur at various scales, from individual buildings or factories to regional utilities or multinational supply chains. Many industry associations and regulatory agencies publish water use benchmarks for key sectors, providing a valuable reference point for performance assessment.

Best practice identification is a core benefit of benchmarking. By studying the systems, processes, and cultures of high-performing organizations, others can adopt, adapt, or leapfrog to more efficient models. Best practices might include:

- Advanced metering infrastructure and digital controls.
- Leak detection and rapid repair protocols.
- Water reuse and recycling systems.
- Demand management strategies, such as dynamic pricing or public engagement.
- Certification or sustainability reporting frameworks.

Organizations serious about water stewardship use benchmarking not just as a reporting requirement, but as an ongoing management tool. Internal benchmarking across business units or facilities can reveal "quick wins" or low-hanging fruit, while external benchmarking may spark more ambitious, strategic shifts.

Digitalization for Water Management

The digital transformation of water management is unlocking powerful new capabilities for measurement, analysis, and operational control. Digital technologies enable real-time data collection, remote monitoring, automated response, and advanced analytics, turning water systems into smart, responsive networks.

IoT Sensors, SCADA, and Data Analytics

Internet of Things (IoT) sensors are revolutionizing the monitoring of water infrastructure, equipment, and natural systems. These sensors measure variables such as flow, pressure, temperature, level, quality (e.g., pH, turbidity, conductivity), and can be deployed at key points throughout water supply and distribution systems, treatment plants, agricultural fields, industrial processes, and buildings.

SCADA systems collect, transmit, and analyze data from hundreds or thousands of sensors, integrating information from diverse sources into centralized control rooms or cloud platforms. Operators gain a holistic, real-time view of water use, system health, and environmental conditions.

With the explosion of data comes the ability to leverage **advanced analytics**, including:

- **Trend analysis:** Identifying seasonal, daily, or abnormal patterns in water use.
- **Predictive modeling:** Anticipating equipment failures, leaks, or demand spikes before they occur.
- **Anomaly detection:** Flagging unexpected changes in flow, pressure, or quality that may indicate leaks, tampering, or contamination.
- **Optimization algorithms:** Recommending operational adjustments, such as pump schedules, valve settings, or irrigation intervals, to maximize efficiency and minimize costs.

For industrial facilities, digitalization supports fine-grained tracking of process water use, closed-loop systems, and compliance with increasingly complex permits. In municipal utilities, SCADA and IoT provide early warning of main breaks, theft, or deteriorating water quality, while supporting demand forecasting, asset management, and emergency response.

For agriculture, digital tools enable **precision irrigation**, integrating sensor data on soil moisture, weather forecasts, crop growth, and evapotranspiration to deliver exactly the right amount of water at the right time.

Digitalization also enhances **collaboration and transparency**, data can be shared with regulators, customers, supply chain partners, or the public, building trust and accountability.

Remote Metering and Real-Time Feedback

Remote metering (also called Advanced Metering Infrastructure, AMI) automates the collection of water use data from meters installed in homes, businesses, factories, or fields. Unlike traditional manual readings, AMI enables:

- Frequent or continuous data capture (hourly, daily, or even in real time).
- Automatic transmission to central databases via wireless, cellular, or satellite networks.
- Immediate detection of leaks, abnormal use, or meter tampering.

For utilities, remote metering reduces labor costs, eliminates human error, and enables flexible billing based on actual consumption. Customers can access detailed, up-to-date information on their usage patterns via web portals or mobile apps, empowering them to make informed decisions and respond quickly to leaks or overuse.

Real-time feedback closes the loop between measurement and behavior change. When customers or operators receive timely alerts, such as spikes in usage, comparisons with peers, or progress toward conservation goals, they are more likely to take prompt, effective action.

Examples of real-time feedback mechanisms include:

- **Leak alerts:** Notifying property owners of suspected leaks within hours of detection.
- **Usage comparisons:** Showing how a household or facility's water use compares with similar users.
- **Peak demand warnings:** Encouraging users to shift consumption away from times of system stress.
- **Conservation incentives:** Gamified apps, competitions, or rebates based on real-time performance.

Studies consistently show that providing real-time, personalized feedback can cut water use by 5–20%, depending on context and user engagement.

The combination of IoT, SCADA, remote metering, and real-time feedback is transforming water management from a slow, manual, and reactive function into a nimble, data-driven discipline. As costs fall and digital literacy rises, these tools are becoming accessible to organizations of all sizes and sectors, creating new opportunities for efficiency, sustainability, and resilience.

Reporting and Verification Systems

Transparent, accurate, and credible reporting of water use and performance is essential for internal management, regulatory compliance, stakeholder engagement, and market positioning. As water risk rises on the global agenda, organizations are under increasing pressure to disclose their water strategies, footprints, and results, not just to regulators, but to investors, customers, and the broader public.

Sustainability Standards and Certifications

Sustainability standards and certifications provide a structured framework for reporting, benchmarking, and improving water performance. These frameworks often go beyond legal requirements, embedding best practices in measurement, target setting, continuous improvement, and third-party verification.

Key international standards include:

- **ISO 14046 Water Footprint:** Provides principles, requirements, and guidelines for water footprint assessment of products, processes, and organizations, based on life cycle assessment.
- **Alliance for Water Stewardship (AWS) Standard:** A global benchmark for responsible water management, focusing on good governance, sustainable balance, water quality, important water-related areas, and stakeholder engagement.
- **LEED (Leadership in Energy and Environmental Design):** While primarily focused on building sustainability, LEED includes credits for water efficiency, innovative metering, and reuse.
- **CDP Water Security:** A global disclosure system for investors, companies, cities, and regions to manage their environmental impacts, including water use, risk, and governance.
- **Global Reporting Initiative (GRI):** The GRI Standards include a dedicated module for water and effluents, setting clear expectations for disclosure of withdrawals, discharges, and impacts.

Sector-specific certifications (e.g., in food, textiles, mining) often incorporate water stewardship requirements, encouraging companies to document, report, and continuously improve their water management.

The certification process typically involves:

- Establishing a baseline and collecting data across sites or supply chains.
- Setting targets and policies aligned with best practice or global commitments (e.g., SDG 6, the Sustainable Development Goal for water and sanitation).
- Implementing improvements and tracking results.
- Undergoing independent audits and submitting documentation for review.
- Achieving, maintaining, and publicly communicating certification status.

Beyond compliance and reporting, certification can confer tangible benefits: reduced regulatory risk, preferential market access, enhanced reputation, and the ability to attract investment or project finance linked to sustainability performance.

Public Disclosure and Accountability

Public disclosure of water data and performance is increasingly expected, and in some jurisdictions, required, of organizations with significant water footprints or risks. Disclosure serves multiple purposes:

- Building trust with local communities, regulators, and civil society.
- Enabling informed decision-making by investors, customers, and partners.
- Facilitating benchmarking, peer learning, and market competition.
- Exposing gaps, weaknesses, or opportunities for improvement.

Best practice disclosure is clear, comprehensive, and timely. It typically includes:

- **Absolute and intensity-based water use data:** Total withdrawals, discharges, and consumption, normalized by production, revenue, or other denominators.
- **Risk assessment:** Identification of operations in water-stressed or high-risk areas.
- **Targets and progress:** Quantified goals for reduction, reuse, and stewardship, and regular reporting on achievements and setbacks.
- **Engagement activities:** Collaboration with stakeholders, participation in catchment or basin management, and support for collective action.
- **Impact narratives:** Stories, case examples, and testimonials that illustrate both quantitative and qualitative results.

Accountability mechanisms strengthen disclosure by tying water performance to executive compensation, supply chain contracts, or community benefit agreements. Some organizations publish detailed water stewardship reports, undergo external assurance, or participate in multi-stakeholder review panels.

Digital platforms are increasingly being used for disclosure, making data accessible, interactive, and comparable. Tools such as online dashboards, open data portals, and GIS-based mapping enhance transparency and enable users to drill down to site-level information or analyze trends over time.

Challenges and opportunities:

- Accurate data collection and reporting require investment in monitoring, IT, and training.
- Balancing commercial confidentiality with transparency can be difficult, especially in competitive or regulated industries.
- Third-party verification adds credibility, but can increase cost and complexity.

In summary, robust reporting and verification systems close the loop between measurement, action, and accountability. They support continuous improvement, stakeholder engagement, and the emergence of a global culture of water stewardship.

Conclusion

Integrated monitoring and performance metrics are the foundation of effective water conservation and efficiency across all sectors. By embracing water audits, KPIs, benchmarking, digital tools, and transparent reporting, organizations can drive step-change improvements, anticipate and manage risks, and demonstrate leadership in the stewardship of one of the world's most vital resources. As the digital revolution accelerates and societal expectations rise, the future of water management will be defined by those who measure better, manage smarter, and share results openly.

Chapter 7 – Policy Instruments and Regulatory Approaches

Water conservation and efficiency do not happen in a policy vacuum. The frameworks, rules, incentives, and support mechanisms crafted by governments and regulators fundamentally shape how water is valued, managed, and shared across society. Effective policy instruments serve as both the guardrails and the catalysts for better water use, creating the conditions under which innovation, investment, and collaboration can flourish. As water stress intensifies and the demands on finite resources multiply, robust and adaptive policy approaches are more essential than ever.

This chapter examines the diverse suite of policy instruments available to drive water efficiency and conservation across all major sectors. Regulatory tools, such as abstraction limits, licensing systems, and sector-specific mandates, define who can use water, in what quantities, and under what conditions. These rules set clear expectations, prevent overuse, and ensure that essential needs and ecosystem requirements are protected.

Yet, regulation alone is rarely sufficient. Economic and market-based instruments, such as water pricing, tariffs, taxes, and tradable water rights, introduce powerful incentives for efficiency and help allocate water to its highest-value uses. When thoughtfully designed, these mechanisms encourage users to invest in conservation, reduce waste, and adopt best practices.

Recognizing that not all users have equal capacity to change, the chapter also explores innovation incentives and compliance support. Rebates, grants, research and development funding, and technical assistance programs help lower barriers and accelerate the uptake of water-saving technologies and behaviors, especially among small businesses and vulnerable communities.

By weaving together regulatory requirements, economic signals, and enabling support, integrated policy approaches can unlock widespread and sustained improvements in water management. This chapter provides a comprehensive overview of how policy and regulation, aligned with broader sustainability goals, are indispensable tools for securing a resilient water future.

Regulatory Tools for Water Efficiency

Regulation is the foundation of effective water management, establishing clear rules of engagement, protecting public interests, and ensuring that the needs of people and the environment are safeguarded over time. Regulatory tools come in many forms, from quantitative limits and permitting systems to performance standards and mandatory reporting requirements. Together, these instruments provide the backbone for managing demand, reducing waste, and securing the benefits of water efficiency for all.

Abstraction Limits and Licensing

Setting limits on water abstraction is perhaps the most fundamental regulatory tool for managing finite resources. Without clear caps on withdrawals, water systems can be rapidly depleted, ecosystems damaged, and social conflicts exacerbated. Abstraction limits are typically set by government agencies based on scientific assessments of sustainable yield, environmental flow requirements, historical use patterns, and projected future needs.

Licensing and permitting systems operationalize these limits. Every user, be it a farmer, factory, utility, or municipality, must obtain a permit or license to abstract a specified volume of water, often for a fixed duration and under specific conditions. This process allows authorities to allocate water equitably, monitor cumulative impacts, and adapt to changing circumstances such as drought, population growth, or emerging industries.

Key features of effective abstraction licensing frameworks include:

- **Quantitative allocation:** Permits specify maximum allowable withdrawal volumes, often by season, source, or use type.
- **Priority ranking:** Critical uses (such as drinking water, sanitation, and basic food production) are prioritized, with lower-priority uses subject to restrictions during scarcity.
- **Monitoring and compliance:** License holders are required to meter and report usage, and authorities conduct periodic audits or inspections to verify compliance.
- **Adaptability:** Licenses may be adjusted, suspended, or revoked in response to changing conditions or non-compliance.
- **Public participation:** Transparent decision-making and opportunities for stakeholder input help build legitimacy and trust in the system.

In water-scarce regions, licensing also provides the legal foundation for water markets, trading schemes, or reallocation to higher-value uses. Without robust licensing, informal or illegal withdrawals can proliferate, undermining sustainability and equity.

Sector-Specific Efficiency Mandates

Beyond limiting overall withdrawals, many governments have introduced sector-specific mandates that require or incentivize the adoption of water-efficient practices, technologies, or processes. These mandates may be embedded in law, regulation, or policy, and are particularly impactful in high-demand sectors such as agriculture, industry, and urban utilities.

Agriculture remains the largest global water user, and thus a primary target for efficiency mandates. Common approaches include:

- **Irrigation standards:** Mandating the use of drip, sprinkler, or other high-efficiency irrigation technologies for specific crops or regions.

- **Crop water requirements:** Requiring the selection of less water-intensive crops or adoption of crop rotation practices in areas facing acute scarcity.
- **Soil moisture monitoring:** Enforcing the use of sensors or scheduling tools to optimize irrigation timing and avoid overwatering.
- **Water reuse and recycling:** Setting minimum thresholds for on-farm reuse of drainage, runoff, or treated wastewater.

Industrial mandates may target specific processes (such as cooling, washing, or chemical production), set maximum water intensity limits per unit of output, or require the installation of water-saving equipment. For example, new power plants may be required to use dry or hybrid cooling systems rather than traditional wet cooling towers, or textile factories may be mandated to recycle a portion of their process water.

Urban mandates focus on utilities and end-users. Common measures include:

- **Leak reduction targets:** Utilities must achieve annual reductions in non-revenue water through active leak detection, pressure management, and infrastructure upgrades.
- **Building codes:** New construction or major renovations must meet minimum standards for water-efficient fixtures, appliances, and landscaping.
- **Restrictions on non-essential use:** Seasonal bans or limitations on activities such as lawn watering, car washing, or fountain operation during droughts.

These mandates are enforced through a combination of permitting, inspections, fines, and (in some cases) public "naming and shaming" campaigns. In many jurisdictions, sectoral efficiency mandates are linked to broader sustainability targets, such as greenhouse gas emissions reductions or climate adaptation plans, recognizing the interconnectedness of water with other environmental goals.

The effectiveness of sector-specific mandates depends on several factors: the stringency of standards, the level of enforcement, the availability of technical and financial support, and the flexibility to update requirements in light of technological progress or shifting water risks.

Economic and Market Instruments

While regulations establish the baseline for water efficiency, economic and market-based instruments provide the dynamic incentives and flexibility needed to drive continuous improvement. These tools recognize that users respond to costs, prices, and market signals, allocating water more efficiently, investing in conservation, and innovating when it is in their economic interest to do so.

Water Pricing, Tariffs, and Taxes

Pricing water appropriately is among the most powerful levers for conservation and efficiency. When water is priced at or above its full cost, users have a financial incentive to reduce waste, invest in efficient technologies, and shift consumption to higher-value uses.

Cost recovery is the foundational principle of effective water pricing. Tariffs and user fees should cover not only the operating and maintenance costs of supply, but also capital investments, resource management, and environmental externalities such as pollution or ecosystem degradation. Where water is heavily subsidized, especially in agriculture or industry, reforming tariffs can unlock dramatic savings and free up resources for investment elsewhere.

Block or tiered tariffs are commonly used to protect basic needs while discouraging excessive use. Under this system, the first block of water (sufficient for drinking, cooking, and hygiene) is priced affordably, while higher levels of consumption are charged at escalating rates. This approach maintains equity while creating strong signals to conserve.

Volume-based pricing, where users pay for each cubic meter consumed rather than a flat fee, encourages careful monitoring, leak repair, and the purchase of efficient appliances. Smart meters, remote reading, and real-time billing platforms make such pricing increasingly feasible even for small users.

Water taxes are another economic tool, often levied on withdrawals, pollution, or overuse. Revenues from such taxes may fund resource management, environmental restoration, or targeted subsidies for conservation investments.

Agriculture: Historically, irrigation water has been underpriced, leading to overuse, low investment in efficiency, and degradation of aquifers or surface water sources. Gradual increases in tariffs, combined with support for vulnerable farmers, can drive uptake of water-saving technologies, incentivize crop switching, and encourage land consolidation for more efficient production.

Industry: Rising tariffs encourage companies to audit water use, adopt closed-loop processes, and treat or reuse process water. Taxes on effluent discharge or pollution can also drive the adoption of cleaner technologies.

Households and services: Real-time pricing and digital feedback platforms (such as water use apps or alerts) nudge consumers to conserve, detect leaks quickly, and purchase efficient fixtures.

Pricing reforms can face political resistance, particularly where water has long been considered a free or low-cost resource. Policymakers must balance efficiency goals with considerations of affordability, public acceptance, and the need for a just transition for vulnerable populations.

Tradable Water Rights and Credits

Tradable water rights, also known as water markets or cap-and-trade systems, provide a market mechanism for allocating water to its highest and best uses within a defined hydrological or administrative boundary.

Key features:

- **Cap on withdrawals:** Authorities set a fixed, sustainable limit on total water use in a basin or system, typically based on environmental flow requirements, long-term yield, and user needs.
- **Allocation of rights:** Users are allocated legal rights (licenses, permits, or shares) to abstract a defined volume of water, often based on historical use, investment, or negotiated agreements.
- **Trading platform:** Rights can be bought, sold, or leased on a regulated exchange, allowing users to reallocate water among themselves without increasing total withdrawals.
- **Transparency and safeguards:** Transactions are publicly recorded, and rules are in place to protect third-party and environmental interests.

Water trading has proven effective in several contexts:

- **Drought response:** During periods of scarcity, users with surplus allocations can sell rights to those facing urgent need, ensuring water moves to its most valuable use (e.g., from low-value crops to urban supply).
- **Efficiency gains:** Users who invest in conservation or recycling can sell their surplus rights, generating revenue and encouraging further investment.
- **Flexibility:** Temporary or spot-market trading allows users to manage risk and adapt to short-term shocks without sacrificing long-term sustainability.

Water quality trading extends this concept to pollution management. Point source dischargers (factories, wastewater plants) can meet regulatory limits by buying credits from others who have reduced pollution below required levels, achieving cost-effective improvements in watershed health.

Effective trading systems require:

- Robust legal frameworks and clearly defined property rights.
- Transparent, accessible platforms for trade.
- Strong oversight to prevent speculation, hoarding, or negative impacts on communities and ecosystems.

Trading is not a substitute for regulation, but a complementary tool that can enhance efficiency, support innovation, and adapt to changing circumstances in water-scarce regions.

Innovation Incentives and Compliance Support

Even the most stringent regulations and market mechanisms can fall short if users lack the capacity, knowledge, or resources to comply and innovate. Targeted incentives and support mechanisms are thus critical to accelerate the adoption of water-saving technologies, build skills, and lower barriers for all stakeholders.

Rebates, Grants, and R&D Support

Financial incentives are among the most direct means to promote water efficiency and conservation.

- **Rebates:** Utilities, governments, or agencies may offer rebates for the purchase and installation of efficient appliances, fixtures, or irrigation systems. These can be targeted at households, farmers, businesses, or institutions.
- **Grants:** Larger grants may support retrofitting, pilot projects, or capital upgrades for utilities, industrial plants, or agricultural operations adopting closed-loop systems, digital controls, or advanced treatment technologies.

- **Research and Development (R&D):** Direct funding, innovation prizes, and tax incentives encourage the development and commercialization of next-generation water-saving technologies, such as membrane filtration, smart irrigation, leak detection platforms, or waterless manufacturing processes.

Successful incentive programs are tailored to local contexts, focus on proven or emerging technologies, and are linked to monitoring and reporting requirements to verify savings and outcomes.

PPPs and innovation hubs can further accelerate R&D, demonstration, and diffusion, spreading risk and leveraging complementary strengths across sectors.

Technical Assistance and Outreach

Achieving system-wide efficiency is not only a matter of funding but of information, skills, and institutional capacity. **Technical assistance and outreach** programs bridge knowledge gaps, foster adoption, and build the human capital needed for ongoing stewardship.

- **Extension services:** In agriculture, extension agents and demonstration sites show farmers how to adopt efficient irrigation, manage soil moisture, or select drought-tolerant crops.
- **Industry outreach:** Workshops, webinars, manuals, and case studies help companies understand regulatory requirements, identify savings opportunities, and benchmark performance.
- **Utility programs:** Many utilities offer free water audits, home visits, conservation kits, or community events to educate customers about efficient practices.
- **Digital tools:** Online calculators, benchmarking platforms, and mobile apps provide users with tailored information, tips, and real-time feedback.

Compliance support is particularly vital for small businesses, rural communities, or marginalized groups who may lack resources to navigate complex regulations or access financial incentives. Support may include streamlined permitting, translation of materials, flexible payment options, or bundled services that reduce administrative burdens.

Peer learning and communities of practice create networks for sharing experience, troubleshooting challenges, and celebrating successes. Policy frameworks that facilitate stakeholder engagement, through advisory councils, public consultations, or catchment forums, further build legitimacy and collective ownership.

Outreach and technical support also serve to inform policy, as practitioners relay ground-level insights, practical barriers, and emerging trends back to regulators and program designers.

Chapter 8 – Institutional and Stakeholder Engagement

Water management is far more than a technical or engineering challenge, it is, at its core, a matter of governance, cooperation, and shared responsibility. The diversity and complexity of water users, rights, and impacts mean that no single institution or actor can address water security in isolation. Effective water conservation and efficiency require broad engagement across all levels of government, utilities, the private sector, industry associations, civil society, and individual citizens. Only through sustained institutional collaboration and meaningful stakeholder participation can the full spectrum of water challenges be addressed and durable solutions achieved.

This chapter explores the vital roles that key institutions play in shaping water management outcomes. It highlights how government agencies set policy, allocate resources, and regulate use, while utilities are responsible for the day-to-day delivery of water services and implementation of efficiency measures. The private sector and industry associations, meanwhile, drive innovation, stewardship, and best practice within and across industries, responding to both regulatory requirements and market opportunities.

Public awareness and behavioral change are also central, as policies and technologies achieve little without widespread buy-in and shifts in consumption habits. Educational campaigns, citizen-led initiatives, and voluntary stewardship programs are powerful levers for embedding conservation values at every level of society.

At the same time, today's water challenges are increasingly cross-sectoral and multi-scalar. Achieving real impact demands coordination across administrative boundaries and active partnerships among all stakeholders. Collaborative platforms, regional and national forums, and multistakeholder dialogues enable shared learning, conflict resolution, and the alignment of goals.

By unpacking the dynamics of institutional roles and stakeholder engagement, this chapter offers a roadmap for building robust, inclusive governance structures. Only through genuine collaboration, transparency, and accountability can the path toward water security and sustainable development be realized.

Roles of Key Institutions in Water Management

Effective water management is inherently collaborative, requiring the involvement of multiple institutions with distinct mandates, capacities, and resources. The governance of water spans public and private sectors, national and local governments, utilities, industry, and civil society, each playing critical roles in planning, investment, regulation, implementation, and innovation. Understanding how these key institutions interact, and how their efforts can be harmonized, is vital for achieving sustainable, efficient, and resilient water systems.

Government Agencies and Utilities

Government agencies are the primary architects of national and regional water policy. They set legal frameworks, develop strategic plans, allocate resources, and monitor compliance across sectors and administrative boundaries. Ministries or departments of water, environment, agriculture, energy, and public health all contribute to the water governance landscape, often with overlapping but complementary responsibilities.

Policy development and regulation are core functions. National governments set the overall vision and legal basis for water allocation, rights, and protection. They pass laws and regulations governing water abstraction, pollution control, infrastructure development, and ecosystem conservation. In federal or decentralized systems, state or provincial authorities may hold significant autonomy, tailoring water management to local contexts while aligning with national priorities.

Resource allocation is managed through permitting and licensing systems, ensuring that water withdrawals and discharges stay within sustainable limits. Government agencies collect and analyze data on water availability, demand, and quality, using this information to update policies, respond to droughts or floods, and coordinate emergency responses.

Investment and planning fall within the remit of public authorities, often in partnership with multilateral banks, donors, or private investors. Governments set the framework for large-scale infrastructure, dams, treatment plants, reservoirs, irrigation systems, and monitoring networks. Long-term planning integrates water with climate adaptation, energy, urban development, and economic growth objectives.

Enforcement and compliance require dedicated agencies to inspect, monitor, and, when necessary, sanction non-compliance. Effective enforcement builds public trust and ensures that regulations have real impact, not just symbolic value.

Public utilities, whether municipal departments, state-owned enterprises, or regional authorities, are the operational heart of water supply and sanitation systems. Utilities are responsible for treating, distributing, and monitoring potable water, collecting and treating wastewater, maintaining networks, and engaging with customers. They translate policy into daily practice, investing in efficiency measures, leak reduction, water quality monitoring, and customer education.

Many leading utilities have adopted proactive approaches to conservation, demand management, and resource protection. They drive innovation by piloting new technologies, partnering with research institutions, and sharing best practices with peers worldwide. Utilities also play a central role in crisis response, managing droughts, floods, and water quality incidents with flexibility and resilience.

Increasingly, utilities are expected to integrate environmental and social goals, such as ecosystem restoration, community engagement, and climate resilience, into their operations. Effective governance requires clear mandates, adequate funding, technical capacity, and accountability to both regulators and the public.

Private Sector and Industry Associations

The private sector is a key actor in water management, both as a user and as a provider of solutions. Industries, ranging from food and beverage to textiles, mining, chemicals, energy, and technology, are significant water users, often operating in regions of high water stress. Their decisions and practices have direct impacts on local resources, communities, and ecosystems.

Corporate water stewardship is gaining prominence, as companies recognize that water risks, scarcity, pollution, regulatory uncertainty, reputational threats, can jeopardize operations, supply chains, and financial performance. Many leading companies set ambitious water efficiency targets, invest in recycling and reuse, and work to minimize their footprints. Some participate in voluntary certification programs or align with global frameworks such as the Alliance for Water Stewardship Standard, CDP Water Security, or the Sustainable Development Goals.

Industry associations play a vital convening and advocacy role. They develop sectoral guidelines, facilitate peer learning, and represent member interests in policy debates. Associations can negotiate sector-wide agreements on water use, data sharing, or environmental standards, amplifying collective action and supporting government efforts.

The private sector also drives innovation in technology, infrastructure, and management practices. Companies develop and deploy advanced treatment solutions, smart metering, leak detection, and digital platforms for monitoring and optimization. PPPs leverage private investment and expertise for infrastructure development, utility management, and service delivery, while balancing public oversight and social equity.

Many multinational companies work with suppliers and customers to promote water stewardship across their value chains. Through procurement standards, technical assistance, and financing, they can drive efficiency and conservation far beyond their own operations.

Increasingly, private actors are collaborating with government, civil society, and research institutions to address shared water challenges, such as basin-level planning, pollution reduction, or ecosystem restoration. These partnerships are most effective when based on transparency, mutual benefit, and alignment with public policy goals.

In summary, effective water management requires coordinated action from government agencies, utilities, private sector actors, and industry associations. Each brings unique strengths and perspectives to the table, and together they can create the foundation for sustainable, resilient, and equitable water futures. Building strong institutions, fostering collaboration, and maintaining accountability at all levels are essential for translating policy into real-world impact.

Public Awareness and Behavioral Change

Public awareness and behavioral change are essential pillars of water conservation and efficiency efforts across every sector of society. Even the most sophisticated policies, advanced technologies, and robust infrastructure can only succeed if people understand the importance of water stewardship and are motivated to adopt new behaviors. Over time, awareness and engagement can transform cultural norms, empower citizens, and drive systemic changes that support sustainable water management at local, regional, and national levels.

Educational Campaigns and Citizen Action

Educational campaigns are the front line of efforts to inform and motivate the public about water conservation, efficient use, and pollution prevention. These campaigns use diverse strategies and media, school programs, community workshops, public service announcements, social media, events, and demonstration projects, to reach households, businesses, and communities. The most effective campaigns are continuous, targeted, and culturally relevant, using clear messages and practical tips tailored to local realities.

Core objectives of educational campaigns include:

- Raising awareness about the scarcity, value, and fragility of water resources.
- Explaining the environmental, economic, and social consequences of overuse, pollution, and waste.
- Empowering individuals and households with actionable steps, such as fixing leaks, installing water-efficient fixtures, changing landscape practices, and reducing unnecessary consumption.
- Building support for conservation policies and infrastructure investments by helping citizens understand the broader benefits to their communities and ecosystems.

Schools play a vital role in shaping water-conscious citizens from an early age. Curriculum modules on the water cycle, local watersheds, and sustainable practices encourage students to become advocates and change agents at home and in their neighborhoods. Interactive activities, water audits, science projects, and outdoor learning reinforce concepts and foster curiosity.

Mass media campaigns leverage television, radio, billboards, newspapers, and online platforms to reach wide audiences. Social media offers unique opportunities for engagement, enabling utilities, NGOs, and governments to share information rapidly, respond to questions, and build online communities around water-saving challenges and competitions.

Citizen action is amplified by grassroots groups, neighborhood associations, and community leaders who champion local solutions. Community clean-ups, river restoration projects, rain garden installations, and water monitoring efforts provide tangible, participatory experiences. Such activities not only deliver direct benefits but also foster a sense of shared responsibility, pride, and ownership of local water resources.

During droughts or water crises, timely and transparent communication is crucial for mobilizing the public and achieving rapid reductions in demand. Utilities and agencies often use real-time alerts, dashboards, and water use "scorecards" to show progress and encourage compliance with restrictions. Effective engagement hinges on trust, credibility, and two-way dialogue between authorities and the public.

Water Stewardship and Voluntary Initiatives

While regulatory approaches are foundational, voluntary initiatives and stewardship programs can drive change further and faster by harnessing intrinsic motivations, peer influence, and social recognition. These initiatives engage individuals, businesses, and communities in going "above and beyond" compliance to achieve shared goals.

Water stewardship encompasses a wide range of voluntary actions:

- Individuals committing to daily conservation habits, such as shorter showers, mindful dishwashing, or turning off taps while brushing teeth.
- Neighborhoods organizing collective efforts, such as rainwater harvesting, greywater reuse, or joint investments in green infrastructure.
- Businesses joining voluntary certification programs (e.g., Alliance for Water Stewardship, LEED, or ISO 14046), publicly reporting on water use and efficiency, and supporting watershed projects beyond their own operations.

- Farmers adopting best practices for soil health, buffer zones, and precision irrigation, even where regulations do not require them.

Voluntary recognition programs, such as water-saving awards, "water-wise" home or business certifications, and conservation leaderboards, offer social and reputational incentives. These programs celebrate success, inspire friendly competition, and create visible role models within communities or sectors.

Public-private partnerships are also pivotal. Utilities, governments, companies, and NGOs collaborate to design and deliver stewardship initiatives, ranging from rebate and retrofit programs to large-scale restoration of rivers, wetlands, or aquifers. Many successful campaigns include elements of co-design, ensuring that local priorities and knowledge shape solutions.

Technology and data play an expanding role in voluntary engagement. Smartphone apps, online dashboards, and real-time feedback empower individuals and organizations to track water use, set goals, and measure progress. Community science projects invite citizens to collect and share water quality or flow data, contributing to transparent, shared understanding and advocacy.

Water stewardship also thrives on storytelling. Sharing success stories, testimonials, and before-and-after examples connects people emotionally to the cause, demonstrating the collective impact of small, consistent actions.

Critically, voluntary initiatives must be inclusive and accessible, reaching marginalized communities, non-English speakers, and those with limited resources. Partnerships with schools, faith groups, and cultural organizations broaden reach and ensure relevance.

In summary, educational campaigns and citizen action lay the foundation for widespread behavioral change, while voluntary stewardship initiatives build on this base to drive deeper engagement and leadership. Together, these approaches are indispensable for building the societal values, habits, and partnerships required for water security and sustainability. As awareness and engagement grow, they unlock the transformative potential of policies, technologies, and investments, turning water management into a truly collective endeavor.

Cross-Sectoral Coordination and Partnerships

Effective water management transcends the boundaries of individual sectors, organizations, and administrative units. Water is a shared resource, linking agriculture, industry, energy, urban settlements, ecosystems, and the needs of present and future generations. No single institution, sector, or jurisdiction can solve water challenges alone. Cross-sectoral coordination and partnerships are thus essential for integrated, adaptive, and equitable water governance. They enable stakeholders to align objectives, pool resources, reduce duplication, and innovate in ways that benefit society and the environment as a whole.

Local-Regional-National Collaboration

Coordination across administrative levels, local, regional, and national, is vital for translating broad policy frameworks into actionable programs on the ground. Each level brings unique perspectives, authorities, and resources.

Local collaboration is the foundation of water management, as water is experienced, used, and managed directly in cities, towns, villages, and watersheds. Local governments, utilities, farmers, businesses, and community groups implement practical solutions, leak detection, pollution control, conservation campaigns, infrastructure maintenance, and source protection. Local authorities have the flexibility to tailor interventions to the specific conditions, cultures, and priorities of their communities. Effective local management also builds social capital, trust, and engagement, making it easier to respond to crises such as droughts or contamination events.

Regional collaboration is necessary because water rarely conforms to political or administrative boundaries. Rivers, aquifers, and catchments often cross multiple jurisdictions, creating interdependencies between upstream and downstream users, rural and urban areas, and sectors competing for the same resource. Regional agencies or basin authorities play a critical role in coordinating allocation, quality control, flood management, and ecosystem restoration at the landscape scale. They facilitate joint planning, data sharing, dispute resolution, and infrastructure development, ensuring that decisions are informed by the realities of interconnected water systems.

National collaboration provides the policy frameworks, legal mandates, and financial mechanisms that enable consistent standards and long-term investment. National agencies set the vision, fund research and development, support large-scale infrastructure, and ensure that equity and environmental sustainability are embedded in policy. They also facilitate alignment with national priorities such as food security, economic development, and climate adaptation. Effective upward and downward communication, between local, regional, and national levels, ensures that policies are grounded in local realities while enabling broad coordination for shared challenges.

Examples of successful collaboration include:

- **Integrated water resource management (IWRM) plans** developed with input from all levels of government and the communities affected.
- **Drought and flood response mechanisms** that mobilize resources across agencies and jurisdictions to ensure timely, coordinated action.

- **Joint investment in infrastructure**, such as inter-basin transfers, shared reservoirs, or regional treatment plants, with co-financing from local, regional, and national partners.

The effectiveness of coordination depends on transparent communication, clear roles and responsibilities, robust legal frameworks, and sustained commitment from all actors. Regular joint planning sessions, shared information platforms, and formal agreements or memoranda of understanding strengthen collaboration and accountability.

Multistakeholder Platforms and Forums

Beyond governmental coordination, complex water challenges demand the active engagement of all relevant stakeholders, public and private sector actors, civil society, academia, Indigenous communities, and the broader public. Multistakeholder platforms and forums provide the spaces, structures, and processes necessary for collective action, dialogue, and co-creation of solutions.

Multistakeholder platforms are institutionalized mechanisms that bring together diverse interests to identify problems, build consensus, negotiate trade-offs, and design joint actions. They may be formal entities, such as river basin committees, water user associations, or policy councils, or more informal coalitions organized around specific issues like drought management, pollution control, or water allocation.

Key functions of multistakeholder forums include:

- **Facilitating dialogue:** Open discussions surface competing interests, mutual dependencies, and shared goals. Skilled facilitation helps participants move from confrontation to collaboration.
- **Building trust and transparency:** Inclusive platforms build confidence among stakeholders, especially when decisions

are based on shared data, independent assessments, and joint monitoring.

- **Generating innovation:** Bringing together diverse perspectives sparks creative solutions, whether new financing models, technology pilots, or co-management arrangements.
- **Resolving conflicts:** Forums can act as spaces for negotiation and mediation, enabling parties to reach agreements outside the courts or political arenas.

Examples of multistakeholder engagement:

- **Water user associations** that manage irrigation systems collectively, set local rules, and oversee maintenance and conflict resolution.
- **PPPs** for developing and managing water infrastructure, combining public oversight with private investment and efficiency.
- **Catchment or watershed committees** that coordinate upstream and downstream activities, such as pollution reduction, reforestation, or flood management, benefiting the whole basin.
- **Stakeholder dialogues** during the development of water policies, where industry, agriculture, Indigenous peoples, NGOs, and citizen groups shape priorities and targets.
- **Community-based monitoring programs** that empower residents to collect data, identify risks, and contribute to stewardship.

Critical elements for effective platforms and forums include:

- **Inclusivity:** Representation from all affected groups, with particular attention to marginalized communities, women, and Indigenous peoples.
- **Capacity building:** Training and resources to enable meaningful participation, technical understanding, and leadership from all stakeholders.
- **Transparency:** Open access to data, decisions, and processes, fostering accountability and ongoing engagement.

- **Flexibility:** Adaptive structures that can evolve as challenges and stakeholder landscapes change.

In summary, cross-sectoral coordination and partnerships, across government levels and among diverse stakeholders, are the engine of integrated and adaptive water management. By bridging divides, sharing knowledge, and aligning incentives, these approaches unlock the collective intelligence and resources needed to address 21st-century water challenges. As climate risks grow, competition for water intensifies, and societal expectations rise, robust collaboration and inclusive forums will remain essential for building resilient, sustainable, and equitable water futures.

Chapter 9 – Climate Change and Resilient Water Use Across Sectors

The accelerating impacts of climate change are reshaping the global water landscape in profound and often unpredictable ways. Rising temperatures, prolonged droughts, more frequent heatwaves, shifting rainfall patterns, and intensifying storms are straining water resources and challenging the reliability of supply systems in every region of the world. These changes threaten not only environmental sustainability but also food security, energy production, industrial activity, public health, and the functioning of cities, making water resilience a defining concern for all sectors and communities.

Resilience in water management means more than simply coping with crises as they arise; it demands forward-looking strategies that anticipate, absorb, and adapt to a wide range of risks and uncertainties. Climate change amplifies existing vulnerabilities, exposes new ones, and disrupts historical assumptions about water availability and demand. In this new era, decision-makers must move beyond traditional approaches, adopting dynamic and integrated solutions that enhance the capacity of people, infrastructure, and ecosystems to respond to shocks and stresses.

This chapter explores the multidimensional relationship between climate change and water use across key sectors, agriculture, energy, industry, cities, and ecosystems. It examines the diverse risks posed by extreme events and gradual changes, highlighting how each sector is affected and what adaptation measures are needed to ensure continuity and security. The chapter delves into scenario-based planning, stress testing, diversification of supply, adaptive infrastructure, and the role of nature-based solutions and risk-sharing mechanisms in building system-wide resilience.

By synthesizing lessons from previous chapters and focusing on integrated, actionable strategies, this chapter provides a framework for transforming water management in a climate-uncertain world.

Ultimately, resilient water use is not just a technical goal but a societal imperative, essential for sustaining development, equity, and well-being in the face of ongoing change.

Climate Risks to Sectoral Water Use

Climate change is fundamentally reshaping the availability, reliability, and quality of water resources worldwide. As global temperatures rise, the hydrological cycle intensifies, leading to more frequent and severe droughts, prolonged heatwaves, and increasingly unpredictable rainfall patterns. These climate-driven risks are not felt equally across all sectors. Instead, they intersect with the particular water needs, sensitivities, and adaptive capacities of agriculture, energy, industry, cities, and ecosystems, posing profound challenges for water security, economic resilience, and social well-being.

Droughts, Heatwaves, and Shifting Rainfall

Droughts are becoming more common, prolonged, and intense in many regions as a direct consequence of global warming. A drought is not just the absence of rainfall, but a sustained period of below-average precipitation that reduces soil moisture, depletes reservoirs and aquifers, and threatens water supplies for human and ecological needs. Droughts can be meteorological (less rain), hydrological (reduced streamflow or groundwater recharge), or agricultural (loss of soil moisture for crops).

In parallel, **heatwaves**, periods of exceptionally high temperatures, are also increasing in frequency and duration. Heatwaves drive up water demand for irrigation, cooling, and personal consumption, even as supplies diminish due to higher evaporation rates from soils, water bodies, and reservoirs. The combined effect of drought and heat stress can overwhelm water infrastructure, reduce hydropower generation, disrupt food production, and endanger public health.

Shifting rainfall patterns add further uncertainty. In some areas, wet seasons are becoming shorter and more intense, increasing flood risk while reducing groundwater recharge. In others, traditional rainfall cycles are being disrupted altogether, making it harder for farmers, utilities, and industries to plan and invest. These changes are often compounded by non-climatic drivers such as population growth, land use change, and competition among sectors.

For example, the Mediterranean, Southern Africa, southwestern United States, parts of Australia, and Central Asia are experiencing more frequent and severe droughts. Monsoon-dependent regions in Asia and Africa face growing variability, with some years bringing too little rain and others bringing damaging floods. Small island developing states and low-lying coastal areas are doubly vulnerable, as changes in rainfall and rising sea levels combine to threaten both water quantity and quality.

Climate risks are further magnified in regions with limited infrastructure, poor governance, or high dependence on a single water source. The cascading effects, such as food shortages, energy blackouts, economic disruption, and even conflict, demonstrate that climate impacts on water are not isolated events, but systemic shocks with wide-reaching consequences.

Vulnerable Sectors and Adaptation Needs

Some sectors are particularly vulnerable to climate-induced water risks due to their inherent water dependence, exposure to changing climate patterns, or limited adaptive capacity.

Agriculture is the sector most immediately and acutely affected by climate-driven water stress. Irrigated agriculture depends on predictable rainfall and reliable water supplies. Droughts, unpredictable monsoons, and reduced snowmelt in mountain regions directly undermine crop yields, food security, and farmer incomes. Livestock production suffers from depleted pastures, dried-up watering points, and heat stress on animals. As a result, agricultural communities are often among the first to feel the impacts of climate change, and have the greatest need for adaptation, through drought-tolerant crops, improved irrigation efficiency, water harvesting, and flexible management systems.

Energy production is also highly vulnerable. Hydropower plants rely on river flows and reservoir levels, making them sensitive to drought and shifting rainfall. Thermal power stations, coal, gas, nuclear, require vast amounts of water for cooling; during heatwaves or low river flows, they may be forced to curtail output or shut down altogether. Solar and wind power are generally less water-intensive, but the transition to renewables takes time and investment. Water scarcity can lead to energy insecurity, blackouts, and higher costs.

Urban areas and water utilities face rising demand just as supply becomes more variable and uncertain. Heatwaves increase domestic water use, strain aging infrastructure, and challenge the reliability of water treatment and delivery systems. Cities that rely on a single reservoir or river are especially exposed, as are rapidly growing megacities where water demand consistently outstrips supply.

Industrial sectors, from food and beverage to textiles, mining, and chemicals, rely on consistent water supplies for processing, cooling, cleaning, and product formulation. Interruptions caused by drought, water restrictions, or poor water quality can disrupt production, damage equipment, and cause financial losses.

Ecosystems and biodiversity are often overlooked, but deeply affected. Wetlands, rivers, lakes, and groundwater-dependent ecosystems provide vital services, flood regulation, water purification, climate moderation, habitat provision, that underpin both human and natural systems. As climate change alters water regimes, these ecosystems face shrinking habitats, loss of species, and reduced resilience, with knock-on effects for all other sectors.

Adaptation needs are urgent and multi-dimensional. Each sector must assess its exposure and vulnerability, plan for a wider range of future scenarios, and invest in flexible, robust, and resilient systems. This may include diversifying water sources, enhancing storage and reuse, adopting nature-based solutions, strengthening early warning and crisis response, and improving governance and cross-sectoral collaboration. Equally important are investments in data, forecasting, stakeholder engagement, and capacity building, ensuring that all actors are equipped to anticipate and respond to evolving risks.

In summary, climate risks to sectoral water use are escalating, unevenly distributed, and deeply interconnected. Addressing them requires integrated approaches that bridge sectors, scales, and communities, transforming risk into resilience and crisis into opportunity.

Planning for Water Resilience

Water resilience, the capacity of water systems and dependent sectors to withstand, adapt to, and recover from shocks and stresses, has become an essential goal in the era of climate change and growing uncertainty. Planning for resilience means looking beyond historical trends and "business as usual," proactively preparing for a future defined by variability, extremes, and rapid change. Effective water resilience planning requires a combination of robust analysis, scenario thinking, investment in flexible infrastructure, and a commitment to continuous learning and adaptation.

Scenario-Based Planning and Stress Testing

Traditional water management has often relied on historical records, assuming that the future will resemble the past. However, climate change, demographic shifts, technological advances, and evolving social expectations have rendered these assumptions unreliable. Scenario-based planning is a response to this uncertainty, a structured process that explores a range of plausible futures, tests the robustness of strategies, and builds flexibility into decision-making.

Scenario-based planning starts by identifying key drivers of change that could affect water availability and demand. These might include climate variables (precipitation, temperature, evapotranspiration), population growth, economic development, technological innovation, policy shifts, and social behavior. By combining different assumptions about these drivers, planners construct alternative scenarios, such as "hot and dry," "rapid urbanization," or "strong climate action", each representing a possible trajectory for the water system.

Within each scenario, planners assess the implications for water supply, demand, infrastructure performance, ecosystem health, and social well-being. This analysis often involves complex modeling of hydrological systems, infrastructure networks, and sectoral interactions. The objective is not to predict the future, but to identify vulnerabilities, "no-regret" actions (that perform well under most futures), and critical tipping points where more adaptive management may be needed.

Stress testing complements scenario analysis by simulating the performance of water systems under extreme or compound events, such as multi-year droughts, unprecedented floods, or rapid shifts in demand. Stress tests reveal the points of failure or resilience in current systems, guiding targeted investments, contingency planning, and capacity building.

For example, a city might use stress testing to understand how its water supply system would cope with a "1-in-100-year" drought coinciding with a heatwave and population surge. The analysis might reveal where additional storage, demand management, emergency supplies, or infrastructure upgrades are needed. In agriculture, stress testing might examine how irrigation schemes perform under scenarios of declining river flows and erratic rainfall, informing crop choices and investment in water-saving technologies.

Scenario planning and stress testing are iterative and participatory processes. They benefit from input by technical experts, local stakeholders, and decision-makers from different sectors. Effective processes are transparent about uncertainties, assumptions, and trade-offs, and are updated regularly as new information becomes available.

Diversification and Adaptive Infrastructure

Building water resilience also requires diversification, of water sources, supply systems, storage options, and management approaches. Relying too heavily on a single source, technology, or infrastructure component exposes communities, industries, and ecosystems to heightened risk when conditions change or crises strike.

Diversification of water sources may include:

- **Surface water and groundwater integration:** Blending supplies from rivers, lakes, and aquifers to smooth out variability and buffer against drought.
- **Rainwater harvesting:** Collecting and storing rainwater from rooftops or urban surfaces for non-potable uses, irrigation, or emergency supply.
- **Water reuse and recycling:** Treating wastewater for reuse in agriculture, industry, landscape irrigation, or even potable applications, reducing pressure on freshwater sources.
- **Desalination:** Converting seawater or brackish groundwater into drinking water, particularly in coastal or arid regions, while managing the associated energy and environmental costs.

Adaptive infrastructure goes beyond traditional "hard" engineering, dams, reservoirs, canals, toward more flexible, modular, and nature-based solutions. Adaptive infrastructure is designed to function under a wide range of conditions, to be easily modified or expanded, and to provide co-benefits for communities and the environment.

Key elements include:

- **Modular and scalable systems:** Water treatment plants, pumping stations, and storage facilities that can be upgraded or reconfigured as demand shifts or new challenges arise.
- **Decentralized networks:** Distributed systems such as local rainwater tanks, neighborhood-scale recycling, or community wells, which increase redundancy and reduce system-wide vulnerability.
- **Green and blue infrastructure:** Restoring wetlands, rivers, and floodplains; constructing green roofs and permeable pavements; planting urban forests and vegetated swales. These nature-based solutions absorb excess rainfall, filter pollutants, recharge groundwater, reduce heat, and create habitat, all while supporting water security and climate adaptation.
- **Smart systems and digital monitoring:** Sensors, real-time data, and automated controls enable operators to optimize water flows, anticipate disruptions, and respond rapidly to emerging threats.

Adaptive management is the governance dimension of resilient water systems. It emphasizes learning by doing, flexibility, and rapid feedback. Managers continuously monitor system performance, evaluate outcomes, and adjust operations or policies as conditions evolve. Effective adaptive management depends on strong institutions, clear communication, stakeholder engagement, and a willingness to innovate and accept uncertainty.

The process of diversification and adaptation must be equitable. Vulnerable groups, such as rural communities, informal settlements, or marginalized populations, often have the least access to diversified water options and the greatest exposure to risk. Inclusive planning, investment in local capacity, and partnership with community organizations are essential to ensure that resilience-building efforts do not exacerbate existing inequalities.

In summary, planning for water resilience in a changing world requires both rigorous scenario-based analysis and investment in diversified, adaptive infrastructure. By anticipating a range of futures, testing system performance, and building flexible, robust, and inclusive solutions, societies can protect themselves from the shocks and stresses that climate change and other uncertainties will bring. This proactive approach turns risk into opportunity, ensuring that water systems continue to sustain people, economies, and nature, no matter what the future holds.

Enhancing System-Wide Resilience

System-wide resilience in water management is the ability of interconnected water systems and the sectors they support to anticipate, absorb, adapt to, and rapidly recover from disruptions, be they climate-related, technological, or socio-economic. Achieving resilience at this scale means moving beyond the piecemeal or sector-specific responses of the past toward integrated, multi-layered strategies. Two critical dimensions in enhancing system-wide resilience are leveraging nature-based solutions and storage, and developing risk sharing and contingency planning mechanisms.

Nature-Based Solutions and Storage

Nature-based solutions (NBS) are approaches that work with and enhance natural processes to address societal challenges, including water security, climate resilience, and ecosystem restoration. Instead of relying solely on built or "grey" infrastructure, NBS offer cost-effective, flexible, and sustainable ways to manage water resources while delivering a host of co-benefits for communities and biodiversity.

Wetlands restoration and protection is a flagship NBS for water resilience. Wetlands act as natural sponges, storing excess rainfall, recharging groundwater, filtering pollutants, and buffering against both floods and droughts. Restoring degraded wetlands or protecting existing ones improves water quality, increases local storage capacity, and enhances the resilience of both human and ecological systems.

Reforestation and watershed management in upland areas stabilize soils, reduce erosion, regulate streamflow, and moderate local climates. Healthy forests and riparian buffers slow runoff, enhance infiltration, and sustain baseflows during dry periods, all of which are essential for downstream water users.

Urban green infrastructure, such as green roofs, permeable pavements, rain gardens, and bioswales, mitigates flood risk, improves urban microclimates, and reduces the pressure on sewer and stormwater systems. These interventions also provide recreational spaces, improve air quality, and support urban biodiversity.

Floodplain reconnection and river restoration restore the natural storage and conveyance capacity of river systems. Allowing rivers to meander and reconnect with their floodplains dissipates flood energy, recharges aquifers, and sustains agriculture and fisheries. These strategies are increasingly adopted as part of "room for the river" programs in flood-prone countries.

Enhancing storage, both natural and built, is central to resilience. Beyond dams and reservoirs, managed aquifer recharge (MAR) uses periods of excess surface water to replenish groundwater supplies for use during dry periods. Small-scale water storage, such as farm ponds, rainwater harvesting tanks, and community cisterns, adds redundancy and flexibility to local systems.

Nature-based solutions are often more adaptive and scalable than hard infrastructure, but their success depends on good design, ongoing management, stakeholder buy-in, and appropriate monitoring. Integrating NBS with traditional storage, such as reservoirs or tanks, creates a hybrid system that spreads risk, extends operational flexibility, and enhances overall resilience.

Risk Sharing and Contingency Planning

No matter how robust a water system is, uncertainties and shocks are inevitable. Droughts, floods, infrastructure failures, economic downturns, or social unrest can disrupt supplies and expose vulnerabilities. Risk sharing and contingency planning are essential tools for preparing for, responding to, and recovering from such events.

Risk sharing involves distributing the impacts of water-related shocks across sectors, regions, and stakeholder groups, thereby reducing the burden on any one entity and enabling a coordinated response. This can take many forms:

- **Insurance schemes**: Drought or flood insurance pools spread financial risk among participants, enabling faster recovery for affected farmers, utilities, or communities.
- **Water banks and mutual aid agreements**: Water users pool resources or rights, allowing withdrawals or transfers during emergencies in exchange for future contributions or repayments.
- **Public-private partnerships**: Risk is shared between government and private sector through joint investments, performance guarantees, and cost-sharing arrangements for critical infrastructure.
- **Cross-sectoral compacts**: Agreements between urban, agricultural, industrial, and environmental interests on priority allocations and voluntary reductions during shortages.

Risk sharing depends on trust, transparency, and clear rules for allocation, compensation, and dispute resolution. Successful mechanisms align incentives for conservation and reward proactive management, reducing the temptation to overuse or free-ride on the system.

Contingency planning is the systematic preparation for a range of disruptive events, ensuring that systems can pivot quickly and effectively when needed. Key components include:

- **Early warning systems**: Monitoring networks, data analytics, and communications platforms that detect and alert stakeholders to impending risks, such as declining reservoir levels, contamination events, or extreme weather.
- **Scenario-based response plans**: Pre-defined strategies for drought, flood, or contamination, detailing roles, responsibilities, communication protocols, and emergency supply measures.
- **Stockpiling and redundancy**: Maintaining reserves of critical supplies, such as water treatment chemicals, spare parts, or portable pumps, and ensuring backup power or alternative supply routes.
- **Training and drills**: Regular exercises to test preparedness, coordination, and response capacity among all stakeholders.
- **Public communication and engagement**: Clear, timely information and guidance for the public, businesses, and vulnerable groups before, during, and after crises.

Contingency planning is an ongoing, iterative process, updated as new risks emerge and lessons are learned. The most resilient systems are those that continually review, test, and refine their plans in partnership with all affected stakeholders.

In summary, enhancing system-wide resilience depends on harnessing the power of nature-based solutions and storage, while institutionalizing robust risk sharing and contingency planning. These strategies, when combined, create flexible, adaptive, and collaborative systems that can withstand shocks, recover swiftly, and support long-term sustainability and well-being for people and ecosystems alike.

Conclusion

As this book has demonstrated, achieving water conservation and efficiency is a cross-cutting challenge that demands cooperation, innovation, and commitment from every sector of society. The journey toward sustainable water management is ongoing, shaped by evolving risks, technological advances, and the imperative for resilient systems. In the final analysis, only through integrated strategies, combining strong policy frameworks, robust monitoring, inclusive partnerships, and a culture of stewardship, can we secure water for people, economies, and ecosystems. This conclusion distills the key lessons and actions needed to move from ambition to impactful, collective water sustainability.

Summary of Cross-Sectoral Efficiency Strategies

Water conservation and efficiency are not isolated technical exercises, they are multi-dimensional, systemic endeavors that span every sector of society and the economy. Throughout this book, we have examined how power generation, agriculture, public water supply, industry, mining, and construction each present unique challenges and opportunities for smarter water use. From deploying advanced cooling systems in energy production to optimizing irrigation on farms, reducing urban water losses, enhancing industrial water recycling, and introducing dry processing in mining, each sector possesses proven pathways to minimize waste and maximize value from every drop. Robust monitoring, benchmarking, and data-driven management provide the foundation for continual improvement, enabling organizations to track progress and identify where further gains can be made.

Crucially, the most successful strategies are those that leverage the strengths of different sectors in complementary ways. Cities can partner with utilities and the tourism sector to drive urban conservation. Industries and mining operations can collaborate within clusters to share water resources and recycling infrastructure. Agriculture can benefit from integrated catchment management, while construction projects can set new standards for site-level efficiency and runoff control. These cross-sectoral synergies not only deliver direct savings, but also create resilience to shocks, reduce competition for resources, and amplify benefits for society as a whole.

The Need for Integration, Innovation, and Policy Alignment

Achieving lasting impact requires more than incremental change; it demands integration, innovation, and effective policy alignment. Integration means recognizing the interconnectedness of water, energy, food, and ecosystems, and designing solutions that cut across traditional boundaries. Effective water management must involve all relevant stakeholders, governments, utilities, industry, farmers, researchers, and communities, working in partnership, guided by shared goals and informed by transparent data.

Innovation, both technological and organizational, is essential for meeting the challenges of a rapidly changing world. Digital monitoring, scenario-based planning, adaptive infrastructure, and nature-based solutions are just a few examples of how new thinking and tools are transforming what is possible in water conservation. Policy alignment ensures that regulations, economic incentives, and support mechanisms are coherent and mutually reinforcing, unlocking investment and accelerating progress at scale. Robust governance, adequate financing, and flexible, forward-looking institutions are the backbone of this transformation.

As climate change intensifies, population grows, and competition for water increases, the imperative for joined-up action becomes ever more urgent. Integration, innovation, and alignment, rather than siloed or fragmented approaches, will define the success of future water management.

Call to Action for Stakeholders

The responsibility for water conservation and efficiency belongs to everyone. Policymakers must craft ambitious yet practical frameworks that foster collaboration and reward leadership. Businesses and utilities should set bold targets, invest in solutions, and share best practices across sectors. Researchers and innovators must continue to push the boundaries of what is possible. Communities and citizens play a critical role by embracing stewardship in daily life and holding institutions accountable. By working together, across disciplines, regions, and interests, we can secure a sustainable water future, ensuring this vital resource remains abundant, accessible, and resilient for generations to come.

www.ingramcontent.com/pod-product-compliance
Lightning Source LLC
Chambersburg PA
CBHW050530240926
51846CB00003B/764
9781991370853